Who Will Be Fed in the 21st Century?

Who Will Be Fed in the 21st Century?

Challenges for Science and Policy

**EDITED BY KEITH WIEBE, NICOLE BALLENGER,
AND PER PINSTRUP-ANDERSEN**

International Food Policy Research Institute
Economic Research Service of the U.S. Department of Agriculture
American Agricultural Economics Association

Distributed by the Johns Hopkins University Press

International Food Policy Research Institute
2033 K Street, N.W., Washington, D.C. 20006-1002, U.S.A.
Telephone: +1-202-862-5600

Economic Research Service of the U.S. Department of Agriculture
1800 M Street, N.W., Washington, D.C. 20036-5831, U.S.A.
Telephone: +1-202-694-5050
www.ers.usda.gov

American Agricultural Economics Association
415 South Duff Avenue, Suite C, Ames, Iowa 50010-6600, U.S.A.
Telephone: +1-515-233-3202
www.aaea.org

Order from
The Johns Hopkins University Press
P.O. Box 50370
Baltimore, Maryland 21211 U.S.A.
Telephone: +1-800-537-5487
www.press.jhu.edu

Library of Congress Cataloging-in-Publication Data

Who will be fed in the 21st century? : challenges for science and policy / edited by Keith
Wiebe, Nicole Ballenger, and Per Pinstrup-Andersen.
    p.   cm.
Distills conclusions of a symposium at the annual meeting of the American Association for
the Advancement of Science held February 2000, Washington, D.C. Foreword, p. viii.
    Includes bibliographical references.
    ISBN 0-89629-704-7 (pbk.)
    1. Agriculture and state—Developing countries—Congresses.   2. Food supply—
Government policy—Developing countries—Congresses.   3. Poor—Nutrition—
Government Policy—Developing countries—Congresses.   4. Produce trade—
Government policy—Developing countries—Congresses.   5. Cash crops—Government
policy—Developing countries—Congresses.   6. Agricultural innovations—Government
policy—Developing countries—Congresses.   7. Soil conservation—Government policy—
Developing countries—Congresses.   8. Agriculture—Research—Government policy—
Developing countries—Congresses.   I. Weibe, Keith Daniel, 1962–   II. Ballenger,
Nicole.   III. Pinstrup-Andersen, Per.   IV. International Food Policy Research Institute.

    HD1425.W48 2001
    363.8'09172'4—dc21   2001038390

Contents

Part IV   Institutional Roles and Policy Priorities

Tables and Figures

Tables

Figures

Foreword

Global food production has more than doubled over the past 40 years, growing faster even than population, and will likely continue to keep pace into the 21st century. Yet one-eighth of the world's people today lack secure access to the food they need to live active and healthy lives. Given the persistence of food insecurity amidst increased per capita food production, the critical question for researchers and policymakers today is not so much *whether* the world can be fed, but rather *who* in the world *will* be fed?

In February 2000, a group of physical scientists, social scientists, and policymakers gathered in a symposium at the annual meetings of the American Association for the Advancement of Science in Washington, D.C., to discuss the roles of science and policy in addressing these challenges. This report distills the conclusions of that group. The authors argue that markets will continue to respond to the demands of those with incomes to spend, in terms of both quantity and quality of food produced and supplied. By contrast, meeting the needs of the poor will require public policies and investments to supplement the operation of markets in three critical areas where private incentives are insufficient: protecting the natural resources on which agriculture depends; focusing the benefits of agricultural research, including biotechnology, on the needs of small-scale farmers in developing countries; and ensuring that access to food, resources, and income-generating opportunities is equitable and secure.

In the absence of appropriate policy measures to address these challenges, food insecurity and child malnutrition will remain widespread in the coming decades. If these three broad policy challenges can be met, however, a food-secure and environmentally sustainable world will be within our reach. We have already made great strides in reducing the burden of food insecurity around the world. Building on the progress made and taking the actions described here should enable us to finally realize a food-secure world in the 21st century.

Per Pinstrup-Andersen, Director General
International Food Policy Research Institute

Susan Offutt, Administrator
Economic Research Service, U.S. Department of Agriculture

John Antle, Past President
American Agricultural Economics Association

Acknowledgments

An attempt to cover a topic of this scope necessarily involves contributions from many areas of expertise. The authors wish to thank Michael Strauss and Bill Ryan of the American Association for the Advancement of Science for their help in organizing the symposium at which these contributions were first discussed in February 2000. The report that grew out of those discussions benefited from the helpful comments of a number of reviewers who read all or part of the manuscript at various points, including Paul Heisey and Shahla Shapouri of the Economic Research Service, Sara Scherr of the University of Maryland, Martina McGloughlin of the University of California-Davis, Pierre Crosson of Resources for the Future, and Agnes Quisumbing and Marc Cohen of the International Food Policy Research Institute (IFPRI). Finally, we thank Heidi Fritschel at IFPRI for her expertise in coordinating the production of this volume.

Executive Summary

In 1960 the world's population was about 3 billion and growing at an unprecedented 2 percent per year, generating renewed concerns about Malthus' predictions some 160 years earlier that population growth would inevitably outpace food production. Forty years later, the world's population has doubled, but food production has increased even faster. Even so, more than one-eighth of the world's people remain food insecure (that is, chronically undernourished). It is increasingly apparent that each of these trends, rather than being deterministically exponential or linear as Malthus predicted, is influenced by market conditions, technology, and policy, and thus by public and private choices. Given the persistence of food insecurity amidst increased per capita food production, the critical question for researchers and policymakers today is not so much *whether* the world can be fed, but rather *who* in the world will be fed? Leaving decisions solely to private choices will provide one answer. Supplementing them with informed public choices and policy will provide a better one.

At present, 791 million people in the developing world (18 percent of its population), most of whom live in Asia, are food insecure. These figures have declined in recent years, from 960 million (37 percent) in 1969–71, but improvements have not been universal. In Sub-Saharan Africa, the food-insecure population doubled over the same period, to 180 million—one-third of the region's total population. Child malnutrition is a particularly important indicator of who will be at risk of food insecurity in the future. About 160 million children under five years of age are malnourished today in the developing world. If they survive, many will suffer from impaired immune systems, poorer cognitive development, and lower productivity. As adults, their ability to ensure good nutrition for their children could be diminished, perpetuating a vicious cycle.

Adding urgency to these patterns, changes in population and income will contribute to increase demand for food over the next several decades. Population growth has slowed, but even so the world's population is projected to reach 7.5 billion by 2020. Almost all of this growth will occur in the developing world. Asia alone will grow by a billion people, but growth will be most rapid in Africa, where the population is expected to increase by 70 percent over the next two decades—even after accounting for the effects of HIV/AIDS. Most growth will take place in cities, which are expected to double in size to 3.4 billion by 2020, representing over half of the developing world's population. As people move from rural to urban areas, they tend to adopt more diverse diets, shifting from coarse grains to rice, and sometimes from rice to wheat. They also tend to consume more livestock products, fruits, vegetables, and processed foods. Rising incomes will also push people toward more diversified diets. Currently, more than 1.3 billion people live on US$1 a day or less per person, while another 2 billion people are only marginally better off. The International Food Policy Research Institute (IFPRI) projects that incomes will increase in all major developing regions between 1995 and 2020, at an average of 4.3 percent annually, although Sub-Saharan Africa's per capita income will remain less than a dollar a day in 2020.

As a result of these factors, IFPRI projects that global demand for cereals will increase by 39 percent between 1995 and 2020, to 2,466 million metric tons; demand for meat will increase by 58 percent, to 313 million tons, and demand for roots and tubers will increase by 37 percent, to 864 million tons. China alone is forecast to account for one-quarter of the global increase in demand for cereals and for two-fifths of the increase in demand for meat. (However, a person in a developing country in 2020 will still consume less than half the amount of cereals consumed by a person from a developed country, and about a third of the meat products.) Can these challenges be met in an environmentally sustainable and equitable manner? Progress will be required both in expanding the global food supply and in improving access to food.

Expanding the Global Food Supply

The total area under crops worldwide grew 12 percent between 1961 and 1997 (0.3 percent per year), to 1.5 billion hectares. However, future expansion of cultivated area will come at increasing economic and environmental cost, so the burden of meeting increased demand for food will rest primarily on improvements in yields. Cereal yields grew 125 percent (2.2 percent per year) between 1961 and 1999, but the average rate of annual growth has slowed from 3.0 percent during the 1960s to 1.1 percent during the 1990s, and future growth may be increasingly difficult. This is due partly to reduced use of inputs, such as fertilizer, reflecting low and falling cereal prices, and partly to low levels of investment in agricultural research and technology. Poorly functioning markets and lack of appropriate infrastructure and credit also contribute.

Given limits on area expansion and increased demands on land already in production, soil degradation becomes a greater potential concern. About 40 percent of the world's agricultural (cropped) land has been degraded to some degree by physical, chemical, or biological processes. While some of these processes (such as nutrient depletion) can generally be feasibly reversed given current technologies and market conditions, others (such as topsoil loss due to erosion) are effectively irreversible. Numerous studies have documented the impacts of such processes on crop yields in specific locations, but extrapolation to larger scales is difficult. Preliminary estimates suggest that soil degradation has reduced global average crop yields by 0.1 to 0.2 percent annually over the past half century. Such losses have historically been masked by improvements in production technology, but they may become more apparent in future if yield growth continues to slow. Yield effects may also be much more severe in particular areas. Advances in spatially referenced data and geographic information system technology offer the promise of improved estimates at a variety of scales.

More limiting than land area and quality may be constraints on access to water. About 17 percent of the world's cropland is currently irrigated, but expansion of irrigated area has slowed from 2.3 percent per year in the early 1970s to less than 1 percent per year in the 1990s.

Challenges associated with resource constraints are not new. Humans have used selective breeding and other forms of biotechnology to overcome these challenges for 10,000 years, modifying plant and animal varieties to suit particular production niches and to provide desirable consumption traits. Recent advances in genetic engineering generate new opportunities in both of these dimensions. For example, biotechnology has tremendous potential to provide genetic resistance to pests and diseases, as well as tolerance to soil and environmental stresses. The first generation of transgenic varieties has been developed largely for crops grown in temperate zones, but genetically engineered varieties can also be developed to address the constraints faced by small-scale farmers in the tropics. Small-scale farmers in these areas are typically least able to combat both biotic and abiotic stresses because of the high cost of pesticide, fertilizer, and irrigation water.

Biotechnology also offers advances in consumption traits. The development of rice that has been genetically engineered to produce iron or provitamin A (beta-carotene) has the potential to directly improve the lives of millions of people who lack essential micronutrients because they are unable to afford sufficient diversity in their diet. The impact of delivering these micronutrients through enriched "golden rice" is parallel to fortifying milk with vitamin D, salt with iodine, or orange juice with calcium in industrialized countries.

While it offers considerable promise, biotechnology also raises important questions. For example, pest-resistant crop varieties can help decrease dependence on pesticides but require careful long-term management. Genetically engineered varieties should not be planted where crops are grown in a relevant center of diversity (that is, where sexually compatible wild relatives are part of the natural ecosystem). Where crops are grown far from their center of diversity, however, as soybeans are in Europe and in North and South America, or as maize is in the northern United States, Europe, and Asia, concerns about gene flow to wild relatives are not always relevant. Biotechnology has also raised concerns about loss of biodiversity. In fact, by demonstrating that wild relatives of crop species can harbor favorable genes that are not expressed in the phenotype of the parent, research in biotechnology provides a strong case for preserving both wild and domesticated forms of biodiversity because of the direct and far-reaching value their germ plasm may bring to future plant improvement efforts.

Improving Access to Food

While expansion of the global food supply will be necessary to maintain and extend recent gains in food security, it will not be sufficient. Equally important will be improvements in access to food, as articulated by Amartya Sen, winner of the 1998 Nobel Prize in economics. Access derives from the ability of individuals and households to acquire food, whether through production or exchange, on the basis of the resources they control. As such, access depends critically on the distribution of income, wealth, and rights, and thus on the performance of markets and other institutions.

Two critical dimensions of access to food are receiving increased attention. First is the role of women as the principal source of agricultural labor, food production, and child care in the developing world. Recent research indicates that improvement in women's education was the single most important factor in reducing child malnutrition in the developing world between 1970 and 1995, accounting for nearly half of the total reduction. Second is the relationship between armed conflict and food insecurity. Recent research indicates that annual food production declined by 12 percent, on average, in Sub-Saharan African countries experiencing armed conflict. In addition to reducing production, conflict also diminishes access to food by disrupting food distribution networks and dislocating populations. Underlying both of these dimensions is the importance of institutional stability and equitable access to opportunities that form the basis of secure and sustainable access to food.

Priorities for Research and Policy

We have argued that the relevant question is not whether the world can be fed, but rather who will be fed. We can be assured that markets will continue to respond to the demands of those with incomes to spend, in terms of both quantity and quality of food produced and supplied. By contrast, meeting the needs of the poor will require public policies and investments to supplement the operation of markets in three critical areas where private incentives are insufficient.

The first area is protecting the natural resources on which agriculture depends. Farmers have incentives to prevent or mitigate natural resource degradation when they expect to benefit directly, but this requires appropriate property rights institutions and access to sufficient financial resources. Additional public support is necessary to address the off-site impacts of soil degradation, including water quality and climate change impacts.

Second is focusing the benefits of agricultural research, including biotechnology, on the needs of small-scale farmers in developing countries. Investment in agriculture is critical to improvements in productivity and food security—both by expanding the food supply (and thereby reducing food prices) and by increasing the incomes of those employed in agriculture. Biotechnology, if appropriately focused on solving small-scale farmers' problems—together with traditional research methods, better agronomic practices, and better markets and policies—can help these farmers to increase productivity, reduce production risks, and increase the nutritional content of their crops. Delivering these benefits will require expanded public investment by developing countries and international agricultural research centers as well as partnerships between the public and private sectors. Governments in developed and developing countries must develop effective biosafety regulations, create and enforce appropriate legislation protecting intellectual property rights, and enforce antitrust legislation to counter excessive concentration in the life science and seed industry. If these steps are not taken, modern biotechnology will bypass the poor, opportunities for reducing food insecurity and child malnutrition will be missed, and the productivity gap between developing and industrial countries' agriculture will widen.

Last is ensuring that access to food, resources, and income-generating opportunities is equitable and secure. Fundamental inequities in the distribution of resources and opportunities will have to be addressed. Broad-based economic development needs to be accelerated, particularly in low-income developing countries; women will need a greater voice in decisionmaking at all levels; low-income people, especially women, will need greater access to remunerative employment, productive assets, markets, education, and health care; and armed conflicts and civil strife will need to be contained.

In the absence of appropriate policy measures for addressing these challenges, food insecurity and child malnutrition will remain widespread in the coming decades. Many millions of people will continue to suffer from hunger and its debilitating consequences. However, a better answer can be provided. If these three broad policy challenges can be met, a food-secure and environmentally sustainable world will be within our reach. Great strides have already been made in reducing the burden of food insecurity around the world. Building on the progress made and taking the actions described here should enable a food-secure world to finally be realized in the 21st century.

PART I

The Challenge

CHAPTER 1

Meeting Food Needs in the 21st Century

How Many and Who Will Be at Risk?

PER PINSTRUP-ANDERSEN AND RAJUL PANDYA-LORCH

Any attempt to address the world's food needs in the 21st century must begin with an accounting of the challenge ahead. Although the number of food-insecure people in the developing world has declined in recent years, lack of access to enough nutritious food remains a persistent problem with devastating human costs. Whereas malnutrition is falling in some areas, it is rapidly on the rise in others. Recent projections show that in the absence of any concerted action to avoid this outcome, many millions of people will still suffer from food insecurity in the first several decades of the 21st century.

About 791 million people in the developing world—18 percent of the population—are currently food insecure[1] (Figure 1.1). South Asia is home to about 36 percent of the food-insecure population, followed by East and Southeast Asia with 31 percent, and Sub-Saharan Africa with 23 percent. However, the incidence of food insecurity is highest in Sub-Saharan Africa, where one out of every three people are food insecure, followed by South Asia, where one-quarter of the population is food insecure. The number of food-insecure people has declined in recent years from 960 million, or 37 percent of the population, in 1969–71 to 938 million in 1979–81, 831 million in 1990–92, and 791 million in 1995–97 (FAO 2000). The largest reduction has occurred in East and Southeast Asia, where the number of food-insecure people has shrunk by half since 1969–71. More modest reductions have occurred in South Asia and in West Asia and

Figure 1.1 Number of food-secure people 1969–71, 1995–97, and 2010

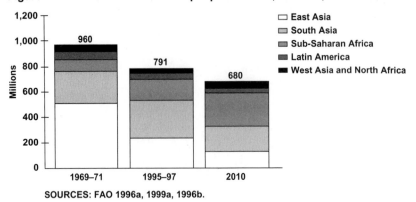

SOURCES: FAO 1996a, 1999a, 1996b.

North Africa. In Sub-Saharan Africa, however, the number of food-insecure people has doubled during this period to reach 180 million.

As to the future, the Food and Agriculture Organization of the United Nations (FAO) projects that 680 million people, 12 percent of the developing world's population, could be food insecure in 2010 (Figure 1.1). Similarly, USDA's Economic Research Service projects that 694 million people in 67 low-income countries will fail to meet their nutritional requirements in 2010 (ERS 2000). Food insecurity is expected to diminish rapidly in East Asia and, to a lesser extent, in South Asia and Latin America, but it could accelerate substantially in Sub-Saharan Africa and West Asia and North Africa. Sub-Saharan Africa and South Asia, projected to be home to 70 percent of the world's food-insecure people in 2010, will be the locus of hunger in the developing world. In fact, Sub-Saharan Africa's share of the world's food-insecure population is projected to quadruple between 1969–71 and 2010, from 9 to 39 percent (FAO 1996a). By 2010, every 3rd person in Sub-Saharan Africa is likely to be food insecure compared with every 8th person in South Asia and every 20th person in East Asia.

Child malnutrition is an important indicator of who and how many will be at risk of food insecurity in the future. If they survive childhood, many malnourished children will suffer from impaired immune systems, poorer cognitive development, and lower productivity. As adults, their ability to ensure good nutrition for their children could be compromised, perpetuating a vicious cycle. About 160 million children under five years of age in the developing world are malnourished (Figure 1.2). A little more than 51 percent of them live in South Asia, 22 percent in East Asia, and about 20 percent in Sub-Saharan Africa.

The International Food Policy Research Institute (IFPRI) projects that,

Figure 1.2 Number of malnourished children, 1995 and 2020

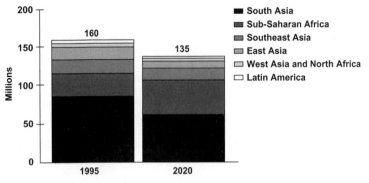

SOURCE: IFPRI IMPACT simulations, July 1999.

Figure 1.3 Percentage of malnourished children, 1995 and 2020

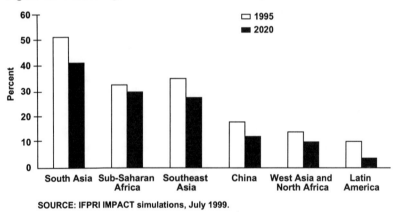

SOURCE: IFPRI IMPACT simulations, July 1999.

under the most likely or baseline scenario,[2] 135 million children will be malnourished in 2020, just 15 percent fewer than in 1995 (Figure 1.2).[3] One out of every four children in developing countries will still be malnourished in 2020, compared with every third child in 1995 (Pinstrup-Andersen, Pandya-Lorch, and Rosegrant 1999). Child malnutrition is expected to decline in all major developing regions except Sub-Saharan Africa, where the number of malnourished children is forecast to increase by about 30 percent to reach 40 million by 2020. In South Asia, home to half of the world's malnourished children, the number of malnourished children is projected to decline by 18 million between 1995 and 2020, but the incidence of malnutrition is so high that, even with this reduction, two out of five children could remain malnourished in 2020 (Figure

1.3). With more than 77 percent of the world's malnourished children in 2020, up from 70 percent in 1995, Sub-Saharan Africa and South Asia are expected to remain "hot spots" of child malnutrition in 2020. Many of the countries in these two regions are among the least-developed countries in the world; they will require special assistance to avert widespread hunger and malnutrition in the years to come.

Prospects for Food Demand

Demand for food is influenced by a number of forces, including population growth and movements, income levels and economic growth, human resource development, and lifestyles and preferences. In the next several decades, population growth will contribute to increased demand for food. The United Nations recently scaled back its population projections, but even with these reduced estimates about 73 million people, equivalent to the current population of the Philippines, will be added to the world's population on average every year between 1995 and 2020, increasing it by 32 percent to reach 7.5 billion in 2020. An overwhelming 97.5 percent of the increase in population is expected to occur in the developing world, whose share of global population will increase from 79 percent in 1995 to 84 percent in 2020. Whereas the absolute population increase will be largest in Asia, 1.1 billion, the relative increase will be greatest in Africa, where the population is expected to increase by 70 percent (Figure 1.4). This rate of increase, however, is less than had been projected in the past, partly because of HIV/AIDS, which is ravaging the African population. The world's growing population will continue to exert pressure on food supplies.

Much of the population growth is expected to take place in the cities of the developing world. While its rural population is expected to increase by less than 300 million between 1995 and 2020, the developing world's urban population is projected to double from 1.7 billion to reach 3.4 billion in 2020 (Figure 1.5). By 2020, about 52 percent of the developing world's population will be living in urban areas, up from 38 percent in 1995 (United Nations 1996). The rapid urbanization of the developing world and associated changes in lifestyles will have significant effects on food preferences and hence on demand. As people move from rural to urban areas, they tend to adopt more diverse diets, shifting away from coarse grains such as sorghum and millet to rice, and sometimes making secondary shifts from rice to wheat. They also tend to consume more livestock products, fruits, vegetables, and processed foods.

People's access to food depends on income. Currently, more than 1.3 billion people are absolutely poor, with incomes of a U.S. dollar a day or less per person, while another 2 billion people are only marginally better off (World Bank

Figure 1.4 Absolute and relative population increases, 1995–2020

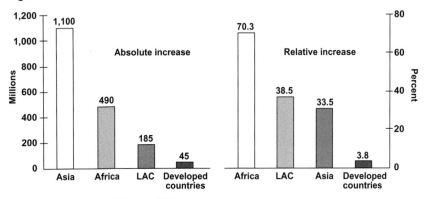

SOURCE: United Nations 1999.
NOTE: Medium-variant projections. LAC = Latin America and the Caribbean.

Figure 1.5 Urban and rural population levels in developing countries, 1950–2020

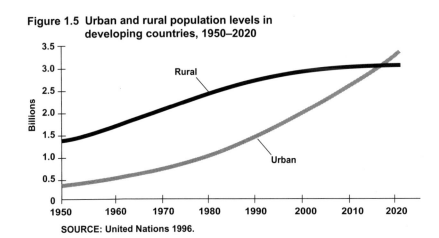

SOURCE: United Nations 1996.

1997). Prospects for economic growth appear favorable in the developing world, and like urbanization, rising incomes will push people toward more diversified diets. IFPRI projects total income in the developing world to increase at an average of 4.3 percent annually between 1995 and 2020, which would double per capita incomes to more than US$2,200 (Figure 1.6). Per capita incomes in all major developing regions are expected to increase over this period. The increase in Sub-Saharan Africa is projected to be very small, however; even by 2020 the region's per capita income will remain less than a U.S. dollar a day, and poverty will continue to condemn many of the region's people to food insecurity.

Figure 1.6 Projected average annual income growth rates, 1995–2020

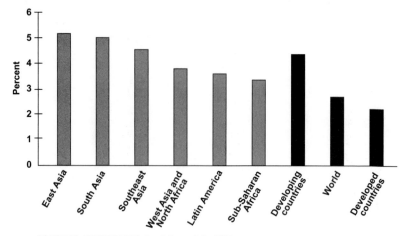

SOURCES: IFPRI IMPACT simulations, July 1999.

Although many millions of people could remain mired in absolute poverty, meeting the food needs of a growing and urbanizing population with rising incomes will have profound implications for the global agricultural production and trading system in coming decades.

IFPRI projects global demand for cereals to increase by 39 percent between 1995 and 2020 to reach 2,466 million metric tons; for meat, by 58 percent, to 313 million tons; and for roots and tubers, by 37 percent, to 864 million tons (Figure 1.7). Developing countries will account for about 85 percent of the 690 million ton increase in the global demand for cereals between 1995 and 2020. Surprisingly, they will account for a similarly large share of the 115 million ton increase in the global demand for meat products over the same period. China alone is forecast to account for one-quarter of the global increase in demand for cereals and for two-fifths of the increase in demand for meat. By 2020, developing countries as a group are forecast to demand twice as much cereals and meat products as developed countries.

However, a person in a developing country in 2020 will consume less than half the amount of cereals consumed by a person in a developed country and slightly more than one-third of the meat products. Per capita demand for cereals and meat products in developing countries will continue to lag far behind that in developed countries, although the gap will begin to narrow in the case of meat products (Figure 1.8). The disparities in demand can be explained partly by lower incomes and greater dependence on roots and tubers for sustenance in develop-

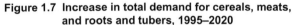

Figure 1.7 Increase in total demand for cereals, meats, and roots and tubers, 1995–2020

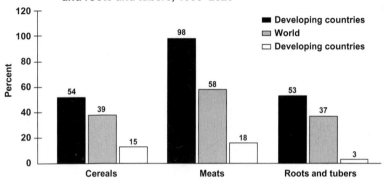

SOURCES: IFPRI IMPACT simulations, July 1999.

Figure 1.8 Per capita demand for cereals and meat products, 1995–2020

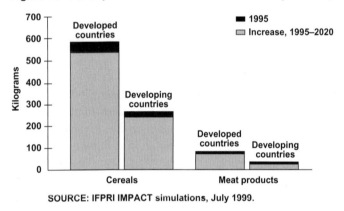

SOURCE: IFPRI IMPACT simulations, July 1999.

ing countries and by much heavier use of cereals for feeding livestock in developed countries. Within the developing world, increases in per capita demand for cereals (food and feed) and meat products in East Asia will far outstrip those in other regions. This is not surprising given that income levels are already relatively high in East Asia and are projected to continue to grow rapidly in the next two decades, triggering massive increase in demand. In the case of cereals, for instance, while per capita demand in East Asia is projected to increase by 66 kilograms, to reach 373 kilograms in 2020, in Sub-Saharan Africa it is projected to increase by only 13 kilograms between 1995 and 2020, to reach 156 kilograms in 2020.

Demand for cereals for feeding livestock will increase considerably in impor-

Figure 1.9 Increase in total demand for major cereal commodities, 1995–2020

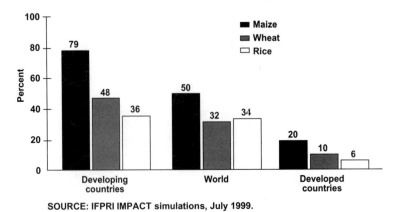

SOURCE: IFPRI IMPACT simulations, July 1999.

tance in coming decades, especially in developing countries, in response to strong demand for livestock products. Between 1995 and 2020, developing countries' demand for cereals for animal feed is projected to double to 445 million tons, while demand for cereals for food for direct human consumption is projected to increase by 40 percent, to 1,013 million tons. By 2020, 27 percent of the cereal demand in developing countries will be directed to animal feed, compared with 21 percent in 1995. In developed countries, the increase in cereal demand for feed will far outstrip the increase in cereal demand for food in both absolute and relative terms.

Because of substantial increases in demand for livestock products, especially in developing countries where primarily maize and other coarse grains are used for animal feed, demand for maize is projected to increase faster than for other cereals in both developed and developing countries (Figure 1.9). Global demand for maize is projected to grow at an annual rate of 1.6 percent between 1995 and 2020, followed by rice at 1.2 percent and wheat at 1.1 percent. In China, where total demand for meat is projected to double between 1995 and 2020, demand for maize is forecast to increase by around 2.7 percent per year, whereas demand for rice, the most important staple for human consumption, is projected to increase by only 0.6 percent per year.

Prospects for Food Supply

How will the expected increases in cereal demand be met? Not by expansion in cultivated area. IFPRI projections indicate that the area under cereals will

Figure 1.10 Annual growth in cereal yields, 1967–82, 1982–94, and 1995–2020

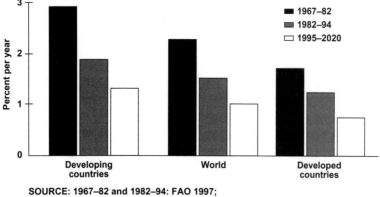

SOURCE: 1967–82 and 1982–94: FAO 1997;
1995-2020: IFPRI IMPACT simulations, July 1999.

increase by only 7.4 percent, or 51 million hectares, between 1995 and 2020, with much of the growth concentrated in the relatively low-yielding cereals of Sub-Saharan Africa. A modest expansion in cereal area is forecast for Latin America, but virtually no growth is projected for Asia or the developed countries. Since growth in cultivated area is unlikely to contribute much to future production growth, the burden of meeting increased demand for cereal rests on improvements in crop yields. However, growth in farmers' cereal yields is slowing (Figure 1.10). This is due partly to reduced use of inputs like fertilizer, reflecting low and falling cereal prices, and partly to low levels of investment in agricultural research and technology. Poorly functioning markets and lack of appropriate infrastructure and credit are also contributing factors. Without substantial and sustained additional investment in agricultural research and associated factors, maintaining, let alone increasing, cereal yields will become more and more difficult in the longer term. The gap in average cereal yields between the developed and developing countries is slowly beginning to narrow. The gap is widening considerably, however, within the developing world, as Sub-Saharan Africa lags further and further behind the other regions, particularly East Asia (Figure 1.11).

With the projected slowdowns in area expansion and yield growth, cereal production in developing countries as a group is also forecast to slow to an annual rate of 1.7 percent during 1995–2020, compared with 2.3 percent during 1982–94. This figure is still higher, however, than the 0.9 percent annual rate of growth projected for developed countries during 1995–2020.

Despite large increases, cereal production in developing countries will be

Figure 1.11 Cereal yields, 1995–2020

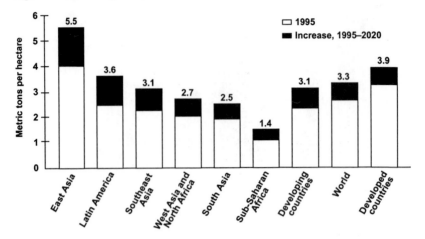

insufficient to meet the expected increase in demand. As a group, developing countries are projected to increase their net imports of cereals (the difference between demand and production) by 80 percent between 1995 and 2020, to reach 191.7 million tons (Figure 1.12). With the exception of Latin America, all major regions are forecast to increase their net cereal imports. The massive increase forecast in South Asia's net cereal imports from 0.3 million tons in 1995 to 20.8 million tons in 2020 will arise because domestic production in the region will not keep up with income and population growth. Sub-Saharan Africa's net cereal imports are expected to remain low because of lack of foreign exchange and entrenched poverty.

Wheat will constitute more than half of the developing world's net cereal imports, but the share of maize is projected to rise from 28 to 33 percent between 1995 and 2020. Trade in rice is forecast to remain small. About 12 percent of the developing world's cereal demand is projected to be met though net imports from the developed world, up from 10 percent in 1995.

About 60 percent of the developing world's net cereal imports in 2020 will come from the United States. With a 34 percent increase projected in its net cereal exports between 1995 and 2020, the United States will continue to capture a large share of the increased export market for cereals (Figure 1.13). However, with the projected emergence of Eastern Europe and the former Soviet Union as major net exporters of cereals and the increase in net exports forecast for the European Union and Australia, the market share of the United States in the net cereal exports of the developed world is projected to decline from 80 percent in 1995 to 60 percent in 2020.

Figure 1.12 Net cereal imports of major developing regions, 1995 and 2020

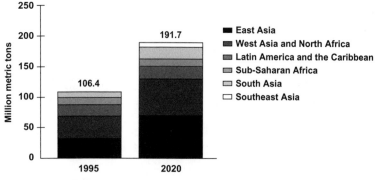

SOURCE: IFPRI IMPACT simulations, July 1999.

Figure 1.13 Net trade in cereal of developed countries, 1995 and 2020

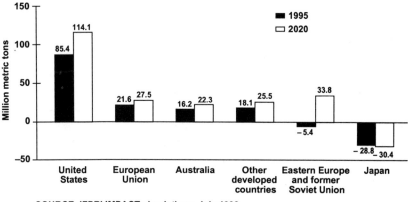

SOURCE: IFPRI IMPACT simulations, July 1999.

With continued population growth, urbanization, rapid income growth, and changes in lifestyles and food preferences, demand for meat is expected to rise rapidly in developing countries. IFPRI projects that meat demand in the developing world will double between 1995 and 2020, to 190 million tons, and increase by 25 percent in developed countries, to 122 million tons. Demand for meat will grow much faster than for cereals in the developing world, by 2.8 percent per year for meat compared with 1.8 percent for cereals. In per capita terms, demand for meat in developing countries will increase by 40 percent between 1995 and 2020, whereas it will increase by only 10 percent for cereals. East Asia's per capita demand is projected to increase most, and Sub-Saharan Africa's and

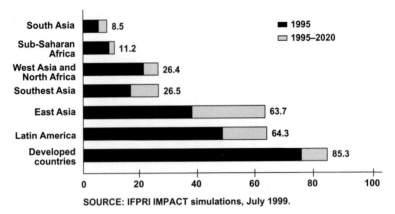

Figure 1.14 Per capita demand for meat products, 1995–2020

SOURCE: IFPRI IMPACT simulations, July 1999.

South Asia's least; by 2020, East Asia's per capita demand for meat could be as much as seven times that of South Asia (Figure 1.14). It is crucial that governments and industries prepare for this ongoing livestock revolution to meet consumer demand while alleviating stresses on public health and natural resources.

Despite high rates of production growth, developing countries as a group are projected to increase their net meat imports 8-fold, from 0.8 million tons in 1995 to 6.6 million tons in 2020. Latin America will continue to be a net exporter of meat, but South Asia will switch from being a net exporter to a net importer. East Asia is projected to increase its net meat imports 28-fold, albeit from very low levels, primarily because of the massive increases expected in meat demand in China.

Net imports are a reflection of the gap between production and market demand. For many of the poor, the gap between food production and human needs is likely to be even wider than that between production and demand, because many of these people are priced out of the market, even at low food prices, and their market demand fails to fully reflect their food needs. The higher-income developing countries will be able to fill the gap between production and demand through commercial imports, but the poorer countries may have insufficient foreign exchange to be able to import food in needed quantities. It is the latter group of countries, including most of those in Sub-Saharan Africa and some in Asia, that will remain a challenge and require special assistance to avert widespread hunger and malnutrition in the 21st century.

Expanding the Global Food Supply

CHAPTER 2

How Critical Are Soil Constraints?

RATTAN LAL

G lobal arable land area (that is, area under annual or permanent crops) currently totals about 1.5 billion hectares (FAO 1996b), up from an estimated 300 million hectares in 1700 (Engelman and LeRoy 1995). The
potential for further expansion is limited because most potentially arable land is
either economically inaccessible or ecologically sensitive. With increasing population, especially in developing countries where land resources are already under
great stress, arable land per capita is declining rapidly (Table 2.1).

Of the current arable land area, about 250 million hectares (17 percent) are
irrigated (Postel 1999). The scope for expansion of irrigated land area is limited
because the land that is most suitable for irrigation has already been developed,
additional land can be brought under irrigation only at high cost, and renewable,
fresh-water resources for irrigation are limited—especially in the arid and semi-
arid regions (Gardner-Outlaw and Engelman 1997). Consequently, the rate of
increase in irrigated land area has decreased from about 2.3 percent per year in
1972 to less than 1 percent per year in the 1990s (FAO 1990). Between 1990
and 2025, the number of people affected by water scarcity is projected to
increase from 130 million to 1 billion (Engelman and LeRoy 1993).

In view of the limited resources of soil and water, future increases in food
production will have to come from agricultural intensification on land already

TABLE 2.1 Per capita arable land area in selected
developing countries

Country	Arable land	
	Hectares per capita	Irrigated hectares per capita
Africa		
Benin	0.28	0.001
Burkina Faso	0.44	0.003
Ethiopia	0.24	0.003
Ghana	0.07	0.001
Kenya	0.07	0.002
Mali	0.22	0.021
Niger	0.42	0.005
Nigeria	0.25	0.007
Senegal	0.30	0.023
Somalia	0.11	0.013
Sudan	0.47	0.700
Tanzania	0.10	0.005
Uganda	0.26	0.001
Latin America		
Ecuador	0.14	0.049
El Salvador	0.10	0.022
Mexico	0.25	0.068
Nicaragua	0.27	0.021
Asia		
China	0.08	0.040
India	0.19	0.051
Nepal	0.11	0.040
Pakistan	0.16	0.130
Sri Lanka	0.05	0.031

SOURCE: Recalculated from FAO 1996b; and Engelman and
LeRoy 1995.

under production. With the world's population projected to be between 9 billion and 10 billion by the year 2050 (Leisinger 2000), there is an urgent need to conserve, restore, enhance, and intensively manage the land already used for cultivation. One of the key challenges facing agricultural intensification in the 21st century is the issue of soil degradation.

Soil Degradation

Soil degradation is characterized by a decline in soil quality or a reduction in soil's capacity to produce economic goods and services and to perform environmental moderating functions (Lal 1993). Three principal processes of soil degradation are *chemical* (for example, salinization or nutrient depletion), *physical* (for example, compaction or reduction in water-holding capacity), and *biological* (for example, reduction in soil organic carbon or soil biodiversity).

The global extent of soil chemical degradation is estimated at 239 million hectares, of which 43 million hectares are considered to be strongly or extremely degraded (Oldeman 1994). Of the total area that is chemically degraded, 135 million hectares are degraded because of nutrient depletion; 76 million hectares, because of salinization; 22 million hectares, because of pollution; and 6 million hectares, because of acidification.

One of the most widespread forms of soil chemical degradation is the secondary salinization of irrigated land. Excessive irrigation, due in some cases to inappropriate subsidies, leads to waterlogging that brings salt from the subsoil to the surface. For example, irrigated croplands suffer from rapidly rising water tables in parts of Pakistan, India, the United States, Ethiopia, Australia, Morocco, and Egypt (FAO 1990; Smedema 1990). Global irrigated land area affected by secondary salinization is estimated at 47.7 million hectares, or 19 percent of the total irrigated land area of 250 million hectares. This includes an estimated 7.0 million hectares (17 percent of total irrigated area) in India, 6.9 million hectares (33 percent) in Egypt, 6.7 million hectares (15 percent) in China, 4.2 million hectares (26 percent) in Pakistan, and 4.2 million hectares (23 percent) in the United States (Postel 1999).

Whereas chemical soil degradation can generally be corrected by addition of inorganic fertilizers, lime, organic amendments, or a combination of these, physical and biological forms of soil degradation are much harder to address. For example, enhancing soil organic carbon is difficult, and increasing topsoil depth lost to erosion is virtually impossible. A decline in soil structure with an attendant severe loss of topsoil depth can have a drastic adverse impact on crop yields in soils with root-restrictive layers at a shallow depth. Severe reduction in topsoil depth also decreases a soil's available water capacity, which cannot be reversed economically in rainfed agriculture. While data are limited, an estimated total of 1,094 million hectares worldwide are affected by water erosion and 549 million hectares by wind erosion (Oldeman 1994). Physical degradation on cropland is estimated at 266 million hectares due to water erosion, 87 million hectares due to wind erosion, and 68 million hectares due to structural or other forms of physical degradation (Oldeman, Hakkeling, and Sombroek 1991; Oldeman 1994).

Soil degradation may have impacts that are on-site (for example, reductions in crop yields) and off-site (for example, impacts on global climate change). These impacts are examined below.

Reduction in Crop Yields Due to Soil Degradation

Soil degradation adversely affects crop yields both directly and indirectly. Directly, yield reductions are due to declines in effective rooting depth and associated reductions in water and nutrient reserves. Indirectly, soil degradation decreases the response to inputs, such as improved crop varieties, fertilizers, and irrigation.

Soil degradation's adverse effect on crop yields may be hidden in the short run because of the masking effect of improved technology. In some slightly to moderately degraded soils, crop yields may even temporarily increase, but at a higher cost of production. In India, for example, the production of food grains quadrupled between 1947 and 1990, and the contributions of Punjab and Haryana to national production of rice and wheat increased from 4 percent in 1950–51 to 21 percent in 1985–86 (ICAR 1998). Yet the area affected by soil degradation increased from 113 million hectares in 1947 to 166 million hectares in 1990, and data collected by the Fertilizer Association of India show that between 1966 and 1992 the incremental response of yields to an additional unit of fertilizer fell by 83 percent for rice and by 64 percent for wheat (Hobbs and Morris 1996).

SOIL PHYSICAL DEGRADATION AND CROP YIELDS

Degraded soil structure reduces crop yields through adverse effects on crop stand and growth caused by crusting, compaction, waterlogging, nutrient and water losses by runoff, and the loss of topsoil by accelerated erosion. Numerous examples of the yield reduction due to these degradative processes are reviewed by Soane and Van Ouwerkerk (1994) and Lal (1998).

Soil compaction affects an estimated 68 million hectares of cropland worldwide, about half of it in Europe and a quarter in Africa (Oldeman, Hakkeling, and Sombroek 1991). Experimental results in Nigeria, the United States, and Europe indicate that adverse effects of soil compaction can persist for several years (Lal 1996b), and that the magnitude of yield reduction can be severe (Kayombo and Lal 1986; Lal 1981a; Lal and Cummings 1979; Voorhees et al. 1989; Håkansson, Voorhees, and Riley 1988).

An inadequate amount of oxygen in the root zone may be caused by crusting, surface and subsoil compaction, water inundation, or other processes. Excessive wetness resulting from poor drainage conditions can lead to changes in nutrient solubility and in the soil temperature regime. Fausey and Lal (1989)

TABLE 2.2 Erosion effects on grain yields for an alfisol in western Nigeria

| Cumulative soil erosion (millimeters) | Grain yield (metric tons per hectare) | |
	Corn	Cowpea
2.6	3.93	0.57
34.4	1.96	0.33
35.3	1.22	0.28
37.4	1.31	n.a.

SOURCE: Lal 1981b.
NOTE: n.a. indicates not available.

found a substantial reduction in yield of upland crops subjected to excessive wetness and inundation in Ohio. Lal and Taylor (1969) observed similar adverse effects of transient inundation on corn growth and yield. Adverse effects of periodic inundation may also occur during the periods of heavy monsoonal rains in South Asia and Africa. Experiments on tropical legumes have shown that transient inundation can reduce nitrogen fixation by root nodules (Hong, Minchin, and Summerfield 1977; Minchin et al. 1977; Wien, Lal, and Pulver 1977).

Reduction in topsoil depth by accelerated soil erosion, along with an attendant decrease in available water capacity and nutrient reserves, is an irreversible form of soil degradation. The effects of severe erosion on crop growth and yield are extreme in soils with root-restrictive layers at shallow depths. Detailed literature reviews (Lal 1987, 1995, 1998) indicate a wide range of methods used to assess erosion-productivity relationships on a plot scale. (While greenhouse experiments and desurfacing studies provide relevant information, the most useful data are those from field plots subject to natural erosion.) Data from plots established in the early 1970s at the International Institute of Tropical Agriculture in Nigeria show that grain yields of maize and cowpea decreased linearly with cumulative soil erosion. Maize yields fell by two-thirds as cumulative erosion increased from 3 millimeters to 37 millimeters, while cowpea yields fell by half as cumulative erosion increased from 3 millimeters to 35 millimeters, as shown in Table 2.2 (Lal 1981b). Similarly, data from different ecoregions of Tanzania show that crop yields were typically about 30 percent higher in the least eroded classes than in the most eroded classes (Table 2.3). On-farm studies in Tanzania indicate that there is a critical value of topsoil depth for each soil, below which yields begin to decline sharply (Kaihura et al. 1996; Kilasara et al. 1995).

TABLE 2.3 Effect of erosion phase on grain yield of corn and cowpeas on soils of different ecoregions in Tanzania

| Crop | Region | Soil | Crop yield for different erosional phases (metric tons per hectare) | | | | |
			Least	Slight	Moderate	Severe	LSD (.05)
Corn	Kilimanjaro	Kirima-Boro	3.4	3.5	3.3	2.9	0.3
	Tanga	Xeno Helena	n.a.	3.0	3.6	2.5	0.7
	Morogoro	Milingano 1	1.4	1.5	1.0	1.4	0.4
		Milingano 2	n.a.	2.5	2.1	1.3	0.6
		Misufini 1	n.a.	n.a.	2.9	2.5	0.2
		Misufini 2	3.5	3.5	2.4	n.a.	0.3
		Misufini 3	n.a.	2.7	2.4	2.1	0.1
Cowpeas	Kilimanjaro	Kirima-Boro	0.7	0.7	0.6	0.5	0.1
		Xeno Helena	n.a.	1.2	1.2	0.9	0.2

SOURCES: Kilasara et al. 1995; Kaihura et al. 1996.

NOTE: LSD is least significant difference; n.a. indicates not available.

Numerous on-farm experiments have also been conducted in the United States and Canada. Results of these studies show a wide range of erosion-induced yield declines in soils of North America. Depending on soil and weather conditions during the growing season, the yield reduction due to past erosion may range from 4 to 86 percent for corn, 12 to 50 percent for soybeans, 25 to 55 percent for wheat, and 22 percent for cotton (Lal 1998). The data in Table 2.4 show a yield reduction of 38 percent for corn and 48 percent for soybeans on severely eroded phase in central Ohio. Similar results from central Ohio were reported by Xu et al. (1997).

It is important to note that soil erosion can also generate gains in crop yields on depositional sites, especially if weather conditions are favorable.

SOIL CHEMICAL AND BIOLOGICAL DEGRADATION

The most severe form of soil chemical degradation is soil salinization. An excessive buildup of salts in the root zone, due to secondary salinization, can lead to a complete crop failure. Risks of decline in crop yield due to secondary salinization are high in Egypt, Central Asia, South Asia, and Australia. Appropriate technologies exist for reclamation of salt-affected soils. These technologies are based on application of gypsum, addition of organic manure, and leaching of excess salts out of the root zone (Gupta and Abrol 1990). Nutrient depletion, such as that widely reported for areas of subsistence agriculture in Sub-Saharan Africa, can also lead to yield reductions. Whereas the loss of topsoil depth by erosion

TABLE 2.4 Grain yield of corn and soybeans for different erosional phases of a Miamian soil in central Ohio

Erosion phase	Grain yield (metric tons per hectare)	
	Corn	Soybean
Slight	7.7	4.0
Moderate	8.9	3.6
Severe	4.8	2.1
Deposition	9.1	3.4
LSD (.05)	2.6	0.6

SOURCE: Fahnestock, Lal, and Hall 1995.
NOTE: LSD is least significant difference.

cannot be replaced, nutrient depletion and acidification can be remedied by addition of fertilizer, lime, and organic amendments, albeit at a high price.

Impacts on Food Production and Food Security

Reductions in the growth of global food production due to soil degradation and other stresses are a potentially serious concern as demographic pressure increases in many parts of the world. The world's 1999 population of 6 billion is projected to reach 9 billion in 2054 (Anonymous 2000). At the current pace, 78 million people are added to the world population every year. Of this, 97.5 percent of the increase in population occurs in developing countries, where the natural resources are already under great stress. The most populous countries in the world include developing countries, such as China (with a current population of 1.25 billion); India (1 billion); and Bangladesh, Brazil, Indonesia, Nigeria, and Pakistan (each with more than 100 million). These and other countries with low per capita land area cannot afford additional losses in their resource bases and food-production capacities.

Because of data limitations, estimates of soil degradation's impact on global food-production are difficult to generate and are consequently scarce. Van Lynden and Oldeman (1997) estimated the impact of soil degradation on productivity in South and Southeast Asia, where human-induced soil degradation affects 46 percent of the total land area. Of this area, 63 percent experienced a negligible-to-light decline in productivity, 13 percent experienced a moderate decline, and 14 percent experienced a strong-to-extreme decline in productivity. The severity of impact is likely to increase under low levels of management.

TABLE 2.5 Estimate of production loss in Africa due to past erosion

| Commodity | Annual loss in production (million metric tons) | |
	Africa (55 countries)	Sub-Saharan Africa (44 countries)
Cereals	8	4
Pulses	1	1
Roots & tubers	9	7
TOTAL	18	12

SOURCE: Lal 1995.

NOTE: Annual loss as of 1989.

Oldeman (1998) assessed the magnitude of the threat to global food security by soil degradation. The average loss in productivity of crops and pastures worldwide due to human-induced soil degradation during the second half of the 20th century was estimated at 8.9 percent, or approximately 0.2 percent per year. On a continental scale, estimated losses ranged from about 14 percent in Central America and Africa; to 6 to 9 percent in Europe, Asia, and North and South America; and about 3 percent in Oceania.

Dregne (1990, 1992, 1995) identified regions in Africa, Asia, and Australia where past soil erosion has reduced productivity by at least 20 percent. Erosion "hot spots" have also been identified by Scherr and Yadav (1996) and Scherr (1999). Lal (1995) estimated food crop production losses due to past erosion in Africa (55 countries) at 18 million metric tons per year as of 1989 (Table 2.5), about 9 percent of production that would be expected without erosion. Production losses in Sub-Saharan Africa (44 countries) were estimated at 12 million metric tons per year, about 7 percent less than would be expected without erosion. Lal (1998) extended this methodology to estimate production losses at the global scale. As of 1995, erosion-induced production losses were estimated at 196 million metric tons per year for cereals, 9 million metric tons per year for soybeans, 4 million metric tons per year for pulses, and 58 million metric tons per year for roots and tubers (Table 2.6). The total loss in food production at the global scale was estimated at 272 million metric tons per year, about 9 percent of production that would be expected without erosion.

Soil biological degradation implies a decline in soil organic carbon, a reduction in the quality of soil organic substances, and a loss of soil biodiversity due to reduction in the activity and species diversity of soil fauna (for example, earthworms). A severe decline in the quality and quantity of soil organic carbon has

TABLE 2.6 Estimate of global loss in production
due to past soil erosion

Commodity	Annual loss in production (million metric tons)
Cereals	190
Soybeans	6
Pulses	3
Roots & tubers	73
TOTAL	272

SOURCE: Lal 1998.
NOTE: Annual loss as of 1995.

drastic impacts both on-site and off-site. Important among the on-site impacts is the decline in soil structure along with attendant manifestations of soil physical degradation and accelerated erosion. In some soils, decline in soil organic carbon also reduces biomass productivity. Important among off-site impacts are declines in water quality due to increased soil erosion and high risks of chemical transport due to the soil's reduced nutrient or chemical retention capacity. Another important off-site impact is the emission of greenhouse gases (for example, carbon dioxide) from the soil to the atmosphere.

Factors leading to depletion of soil organic carbon include conversion of land from natural to agricultural ecosystems, biomass burning, plowing, and adoption of soil-fertility-mining practices based on low levels of external inputs. Most soils lose as much as 50 percent of their original soil organic carbon within 5 to 10 years in the tropics (Lal 1996a; Lal and Cummings 1979) and within 50 years in temperate ecosystems (Donigian et al. 1998). The magnitude and the rate of soil organic carbon depletion is accentuated by soil erosion (Rhoton and Tyler 1990).

Estimating the historic loss of carbon from the global soil organic carbon pool is difficult. Available estimates range from 40 billion metric tons to 537 billion metric tons (Lal 1999, 2000). These losses are over and above those caused by deforestation and biomass burning. Emissions of 66 billion to 90 billion metric tons from the latter sources have contributed to the 32 percent increase in atmospheric concentration of carbon dioxide observed over the past 150 years. These estimates provide an important reference point because an estimated 60 to 75 percent of the loss in the global soil organic carbon pool can be sequestered in soil through conversion to appropriate land uses and adoption of recommended agricultural practices.

The Need for Restoration of
Degraded Soils and Ecosystems

The need to restore degraded soils and ecosystems is greater now than ever before because of the current and projected population pressure on limited resources and the potentially high economic and environmental costs of bringing new land under cultivation. Despite the views of some that "little can be done to restore degraded soils" (Crosson 1997a), the quality of extreme and severely degraded soils must be restored to enhance net primary productivity and improve the environment.

In addition to on-site productivity gains, important off-site benefits of restoring degraded soils include improving wildlife habitat, enhancing bio-diversity, improving water quality, and decreasing the risks of accelerating the greenhouse effect. Restoring degraded soils is an important strategy to sequester carbon both in biomass and in the soil. The biomass produced through planta-tions of fast-growing trees, which has a vast potential, can be used to offset car-bon losses from extraction of fossil fuels. If 200 million hectares of extremely and severely degraded soils can be used to grow biofuel plantations, the poten-tial fossil-fuel offset is 0.3 billion to 0.7 billion tons of carbon per year (Lal 1999). In addition, soil restoration would enhance the soil organic carbon pool, which has been severely depleted through soil degradation. Severely eroded and degraded soils may have lost as much as 35 to 40 metric tons of carbon per hectare (Rhoton and Tyler 1990), and a large fraction of this carbon can be sequestered through restoration over a 25- to 50-year period. The total poten-tial of soil organic carbon sequestration and biofuel offset through restoration of degraded soils is estimated at 1.2 billion to 2.6 billion tons of carbon per year, as shown in Table 2.7 (Lal 1999). This potential is about 20 to 40 percent of the current rate of increase in atmospheric concentration of carbon dioxide. Soil organic carbon sequestration is a cost-effective strategy to curtail the rate of increase in atmospheric carbon dioxide while other energy-related options take effect.

Conclusions

Principal soil and water constraints to enhancing per capita food production are

- a progressive decline in per capita cropland area due to population growth and conversion of arable land to nonagricultural uses;
- a lack of adequate supply of fresh water for maintaining and expand-ing irrigated agriculture in dry regions; and
- severe soil degradation.

TABLE 2.7 Potential soil organic carbon sequestration through restoration of degraded soils

Strategy	Potential sequestration or offset (billion tons of carbon per year)
Soil erosion control	0.6–1.1
Restoration of extremely and severely degraded soils	0.1–0.3
Adoption of recommended agricultural practices on slightly and moderately degraded soils	0.2–0.5
Fossil fuel offset through biofuel	0.3–0.7
TOTAL	1.2–2.6

SOURCE: Lal 1999.

Soil degradation is a biophysical process driven by socioeconomic and political forces. Principal soil degradative processes include accelerated erosion, soil compaction and decline in soil structure, soil fertility depletion and nutrient imbalance, and secondary salinization. Soil degradation is a serious problem in many areas, especially in developing countries of the tropics and subtropics, where harsh climate, fragile soils, and resource constraints make it difficult for small-scale farmers to invest in soil fertility management, erosion control, and restoration of degraded soils and terrain.

A major challenge lies in achieving food security, especially in the tropics, without inflicting even further damage on an environment that is already under great stress. The potential for bringing new land under agricultural production is extremely limited. Just as during the last three decades of the 20th century, future increases in food production will have to come primarily from increases in production per unit of land and water already committed to agriculture. This strategy of agricultural intensification requires increasing the efficiency of fertilizer and water use, prolonging the growing season, and decreasing the risks of soil and environmental degradation.

In addition to soil degradation's impact on current and potential productivity, it is important to recognize links between soil degradation and the environment. The adverse impacts on water quality and risks of accelerated emissions of greenhouse gases cannot be ignored. There is a strong need to create public awareness about the adverse impact of soil degradation on the environment, and about the potential of restoring degraded soils to help improve water quality, mitigate the greenhouse effect, and enhance biodiversity.

Because of these concerns, restoration of degraded soils is a high priority. Although the technology for soil restoration may be known, site-specific adaptation may be needed in consideration of other biophysical, socioeconomic, cultural, and political factors. In this regard, it is important to prioritize regions with a high need and potential for soil restoration. Prioritization may be done on the basis of biophysical (soil, terrain, vegetation, and hydrology) and socioeconomic factors (accessibility, institutional support, and local participation). Pilot projects need to be established on benchmark sites to adapt, validate, and demonstrate the effectiveness of soil restorative technology. These pilot projects can serve as focuses of adaptation through training and through providing material and technical information.

Investment in soil conservation and restoration is a win–win strategy, with the potential to enhance productivity, increase food security, and also improve environmental quality. Soil erosion control would improve water quality and, by increasing soil organic carbon content, lead to carbon sequestration in soil to reduce the risks of accelerating the greenhouse effect.

CHAPTER 3

Is Biotechnology an Answer?

SUSAN R. McCOUCH

Human communities have played a major role in distributing and shaping natural diversity in all parts of the world. For approximately 10,000 years, human beings have modified the traits of plants and animals through the process of artificial selection. As many previously wild species were domesticated to suit the needs and preferences of human beings, the performance and genetic architecture of these species were irrevocably changed. Indeed, most of our domesticated food and fiber species have been altered to such an extent that they are no longer capable of surviving in the wild. Instead they prosper only when nurtured and cultivated by human beings. The interaction of natural processes and human activity has given rise to novel agroecosystems and is responsible for generating and sustaining a vast array of genetic and ecological diversity. Seen as an integral part of the pattern of biodiversity on earth, humans must simultaneously accept and creatively manage the impact of their own species on the planet.

How does plant biotechnology fit into this picture? The term "biotechnology" was originally coined in 1947 and, according to *The Oxford English Dictionary*, it referred to "the branch of technology concerned with the development and exploitation of machines in relation to the various physiological, psychological, and technological requirements of human beings." It was observed that working conditions, lifestyles, and the entire web of human relations were affected by factory work and by interactions with the mechanized world. Thus, biotechnology originally referred to the study of how industrial society affected human beings.

The term evolved into its contemporary meaning only in the last 25 years, and it is interesting to note that humans have assumed a very different role in the new scenario. The second definition of "biotechnology," which appeared between 1972 and 1974, referred to "the branch of technology concerned with the genetic modification of living things to suit human needs and preferences." In this context, human beings have become *subjects* rather than *objects*. Yet, according to this definition, humans have practiced "plant biotechnology" for about 10,000 years, or as long as they have practiced agriculture. From the wild landscapes encountered by early agriculturalists, humans continuously selected and used the most attractive plants for both immediate consumption and as the basis of seed reproduction and plant propagation. They took their favorite foodstuffs with them as they migrated and colonized new lands, bringing novel genetic materials to interbreed with local populations of wild relatives or to crowd out local species altogether. The movement of human, plant, animal, and microbial populations contributed greatly to the modification and diversification of local flora and fauna throughout the world, and provided people with continuously new forms of genetic diversity from which to enrich their diets or better adapt traditional varieties of staple foods. Indeed, human civilization is built on the selective use and exploitation of biological diversity. By learning about the natural world and using that knowledge to shape it in numerous ways, humans have practiced biotechnology both consciously and unconsciously for millennia.

Today, the term biotechnology is largely associated with genetic manipulation at the DNA level. However, it is important to note that not all biotechnology involves *genetic engineering*. Biotechnology may refer to specialized forms of fermentation, clonal propagation of plants or animals, constructing doubled haploid lines, monitoring recombination throughout the genome, augmenting the efficiency of selection in plant or animal improvement, embryo splitting, embryo rescue, and/or protein engineering. A large part of what biotechnology represents today is new knowledge about the natural processes of DNA replication, breakage, ligation, and repair that has paved the way for a much deeper understanding of the mechanics of cell biology and the hereditary process itself.

Yet this new knowledge has brought us to the edge of an ethical dilemma. While the ability to manipulate the hereditary process is not new, the depth of our understanding of this process has changed and the knowledge we have gained has opened up an endless array of possibilities for affecting future evolutionary trajectories. How the potential of the human imagination and creative spirit should be nurtured, guided, interpreted, and ultimately directed and controlled with respect to biotechnology is a question of profound social, economic, and ethical dimensions. It deserves to be discussed, contemplated, and digested at all levels of society.

People want to know why plant biotechnology (as it is currently understood) should now be used in agriculture when traditionally bred crop varieties have provided food for the human population for thousands of years. People also want to know who will benefit from the use of plant biotechnology. What are the risks and who will take responsibility for the problems that are sure to emerge? These are reasonable questions, and they need to be addressed.

Perceptions of Biotechnology Today

Public opinion surveys have demonstrated that, while many people are initially uncomfortable with the prospect of using biotechnology to transfer genes between organisms, those reservations can be overcome if they perceive a particular benefit that they deem ethically or morally persuasive. For example, in a study of 600 New Jersey residents (Hallman 1996), the use of genetic engineering to produce insect-resistant corn was given a 65 percent approval rating, but when the same people were asked how they felt about using genetic engineering to create more nutritious grains to feed hungry people, approval ratings were 85 percent. An even greater proportion (95 percent) approved of the use of genetic engineering of microbes to produce pharmaceuticals such as insulin or antibiotics, where there was a clear benefit to consumers. However, people were much more suspicious about the use of genetic engineering on animals, and most anxious about its application to humans. For example, when the same 600 respondents were asked about using biotechnology to improve the beef quality of cows, only 40 percent approved. A 1997 study by Frewer, Howard, and Shepherd reported that many consumers were concerned about the "trivial" use of biotechnology, especially when conventional alternatives already existed and when perceived risks to themselves or something they valued appeared to outweigh the advantages. The more a biotech application was judged to be useful for society, the more it was seen as morally acceptable. Hallman (1996) noted that "[p]eople want those who employ biotechnology to use its extraordinary power to create products that promise real benefits for consumers, not merely big profits for companies."

It would appear that much of the public could be convinced about the value of biotechnology if those who develop and introduce biotechnological products demonstrated a sincere commitment to achieving socially relevant objectives and were willing to enter into an honest dialogue with the public. Those who stand to profit from biotechnology need to clearly demonstrate that the advantages of any particular product to themselves or others outweigh the risks associated with it and that a rational system has been put in place to ensure the equitable distribution of both the costs and the benefits of the technology. If the public were convinced that biotechnology was being productively engaged as a tool to alleviate hunger and poverty, help small-scale farmers in developing countries, protect biodiversity, help clean up the environment, enhance ecological stability, and improve food and health quality, many people would be far more receptive to its use than is the case today.

Can Agricultural Biotechnology Help Alleviate Hunger and Malnutrition?

While many people enjoy a diet that is more abundant and more varied than ever before, this is in stark contrast to the reality of millions of others who confront profound food insecurity on a daily basis. Food security on a global scale is largely determined by purchasing power rather than proximity to, or direct involvement in, the food production process. As a result, the concerns of the world's poor—who have little voice in the marketplace—are much less likely to be heard than are the concerns of people whose decisions are registered by how they spend their money. While some segments of the population are vociferously opposing the use of biotechnology in agriculture and aim to restrict or completely suppress the use of genetically engineered crop varieties, the potential of biotechnology may represent an opportunity to respond to urgent issues of hunger and malnutrition.

The development of rice that has been genetically engineered to minimize the impact of antinutrients and enhance the uptake of iron and other essential minerals, or to produce provitamin A (beta-carotene) in the endosperm (Ye et al. 2000) are examples of products that have the potential to directly improve the quality of life for millions of human beings who suffer from iron and vitamin A deficiency. People who suffer from malnutrition generally lack essential levels of micronutrients because they lack the purchasing power to obtain sufficient diversity in their diet. The impact of delivering those essential micronutrients through enriched "golden rice" is parallel to fortifying milk with vitamin D, salt with iodine, or orange juice with calcium in industrialized countries. It is not seen as an alternative to maintaining a healthy diet, but this transgenic rice does offer immediate assistance to people in need. Furthermore, as a staple food, rice has a built-in delivery system that is one of the best ways of getting the nutrients to those who most need them. Is it ethical to refrain from using biotechnology to improve the nutritional status of hungry people, while those with purchasing power condone the use of the same technology to extend their life expectancy by producing transgenic pharmaceuticals?

Can Agricultural Biotechnology Help Small-Scale Farmers in Developing Countries?

The use of biotechnology has tremendous potential to provide genetic resistance to pests, diseases, and tolerance to numerous soil and environmental stresses that constrain the production of many crops in both the tropical and temperate zones. Pests and diseases are especially problematic in the tropics because of climatic conditions that favor their year-round growth and reproduction. Acid soils impose a major constraint to crop production throughout much of tropical Latin America and Africa, and, to a smaller extent, Asia. In these regions, small-scale farmers, operating in many diverse cropping systems and growing environments, are typically least able to afford the means of combating both biotic and abiotic stresses because of the high cost of purchasing pesticide, fertilizer, or other soil amendments, and access to irrigation water. The first generation of transgenic varieties has been developed primarily for field crops grown on large acreage under temperate cropping conditions. This focus illustrates the power of large markets to attract the interest of agribusiness. However, opportunities also exist to develop genetically engineered varieties to address the constraints faced by small-scale farmers in the tropics. The primary difficulty in attracting private investment to address the needs of this sector is the small size of each of the potential markets for a specific bioengineered crop variety.

Papaya is an example of a crop grown by many small-scale farmers in the tropics. Crop productivity and quality is seriously threatened by the incidence of papaya ringspot virus (PRSV), for which there are no known plant-derived sources of resistance. A transgenic approach to this problem was pioneered by researchers in the public sector, and PRSV-resistant papaya using resistance mediated by virus coat-protein is now commercially available for use in Hawaii (Gonsalves 1998). In this example, coat-protein genes from a Hawaiian strain of PRSV were used to transform papaya plants, providing a kind of resistance known as "cross-protection." The use of pathogen proteins to provide resistance is similar to the use of vaccines in human medicine. Because it is not economically feasible to manually "vaccinate" individual trees in a papaya plantation, particularly for small-scale farmers, the transgenic approach provided an efficient and economical approach to protection. The resistant germ plasm was commercialized in 1998 and has helped save the papaya industry in Hawaii. Collaborations with scientists in Brazil, Jamaica, and Thailand have resulted in the development of new transformants that are ready to be tested in these countries. Virus resistance is of tremendous importance to many large and small fruit and vegetable growers throughout the world, especially for crops where farmers save their own seed or propagate varieties vegetatively, because the viruses are passed directly through the vegetative material, infecting every new plant in the farmer's field. In these cases, transgenic, virus-resistant material not only enhances yield and reduces pesticide use to control insect vectors, but it also makes it possible for small-scale farmers to save their seed year after year without suffering the devastating decline in plant vigor due to viral infection.

Before any transgenic variety can be released commercially, biosafety regulations in each country must be in place to ensure that rigorous laboratory and field tests are conducted to ensure environmental and consumer safety. In addition, intellectual property rights regarding key components of the transgenic technology often require complex licensing agreements. This can be a formidable challenge to a public sector institution with little experience in negotiating such agreements. In a small but growing number of examples, private corporations have collaborated with national agricultural research institutions in the developing world to extend transgenic technology to crops such as potato, sweet potato, banana, sugarcane, and rice (Rivera-Bustamante 1995; Wambugu 1999). These innovative partnerships between private institutions whose investments have created valuable new technologies and public institutions working to improve the livelihoods of low-income farmers and consumers have the potential to increase returns to small-scale farmers in developing countries and, in the process, to alter public perceptions of the biotechnology industry in general.

Another example of genetic engineering being used to create crop varieties that are beneficial under low-input agricultural conditions involves acid soil-tolerant maize and papaya (de la Fuente et al. 1997; Herrera-Estrella 1999). Plants were genetically engineered to overproduce citric acid in root exudates and as a result were resistant to aluminum toxicity, a common problem throughout the tropics. The high levels of citric acid reportedly acted to chelate aluminum in the rhizosphere and prevented its entry into the root. The presence of citric acid in the rhizosphere also helped increase the availability of calcium, magnesium, and iron, which are normally deficient in acid soils. Plants were transformed with a gene of bacterial origin coupled to a viral promoter, and transgenic plants exuded five times as much citric acid into the rhizosphere as normal plants. Despite the microbial origin of these gene constructs, citric acid production is a normal plant function commonly found in many wild species that tolerate acid soil. The fact that the same mechanism exists in wild plants and in microbes illustrates the ancient origin of the trait and suggests that it is genetically stable.

While biotechnology may be a useful ally in efforts to improve the lives of small-scale farmers in developing countries, lack of essential information about the economic and ecological implications of planting genetically modified crops, appropriate biosafety infrastructure and understanding of intellectual property relationships are often factors that limit the responsible application of this technology. Carefully designed experiments in the field are needed to provide critical insights about the best way to manage transgenic crops in target environments. Restricting the potential to rigorously investigate the field performance of these plants will only create obstacles to the responsible use of the technology by poor farmers. By denying small-scale growers an option to alleviate some of their most pressing production problems with new technology, the lack of alternatives reinforces the use of ecologically disruptive practices among the poorest farmers such as that of slashing and burning forests to continuously clear new land for planting.

Can Agricultural Biotechnology Help Clean Up the Environment?

The use of pest-resistant crop varieties in agriculture can help decrease farmers' dependence on pesticides. Whether resistant varieties are obtained through traditional crossing and selection or through genetic engineering, the resistance itself derives from the presence of specific genes whose expression renders the plant capable of protecting itself from pest attack. Both transgenic and non-transgenic resistant varieties are important tools in a pest management strategy and, if used responsibly, represent an ecologically sound and economically viable way to reduce the use of externally applied pesticides and help to clean up the environment.

While minimizing the use of pesticides represents a critical step toward restoring environmental integrity and improving human health, the long-term management of resistance requires careful consideration. In the context of ecological stability and environmental impact, the use of transgenic resistant varieties should be evaluated from many angles. The possibility that transgenes will be transmitted to wild relatives growing in the vicinity of crop plants should be investigated on a case-by-case basis. It is reasonable to ask whether a specific transgene (or set of transgenes) would affect the fitness of a wild species population if it were transmitted. Where a gene is expressed at considerable physiological cost to the plant, it will be eliminated from a wild population by natural selection unless it confers a real advantage in the wild. For example, a transgene that protects a crop variety from insect or disease attack may be of little consequence if transmitted to wild relatives where the fitness of the wild population is not affected by the specific pest or disease.

Further, it should be recognized that successful transmission of genes through pollen requires the presence of a sexually receptive partner. Many crop plants are grown far from their center of diversity, in areas where sexually compatible wild relatives are not part of the natural ecosystem. This is the case with soybeans in Europe or in North and South America, or maize in the northern United States, Europe, or Asia, such that concerns about gene flow to wild relatives are not always relevant. In cases where crops are grown in a relevant center of diversity and where transmission of a transgene is likely to be ecologically disruptive, carefully crafted biosafety regulations will be required. At the same time, strategies for genetically engineering the chloroplast genome (which would preclude pollen transmission) may provide a way of managing the risk of gene flow.

Can Biotechnology Be Used to Enhance Ecological Stability?

Effective, long-term management of agricultural ecosystems requires a multifaceted approach involving both cultural practices and the use of genetic diversity in a cropping system. Clonal propagation of plants through grafting is a form of biotechnology that has been used for thousands of years, and the more recent application of tissue culture for clonal propagation is now widely used as a way of amplifying reforestation efforts using indigenous species threatened with extinction (Wambugu 1999). Polyculture is also an ancient practice, and offers one way of providing genetic heterogeneity in a cropping system—a well-recognized feature of sustainable agriculture.

Genetic heterogeneity within a single species represents another approach to improving sustainability that is compatible with intensive, high-input agricultural production (Zhu et al. 2000). To construct genetic mosaics that can be systematically assembled into viable multiline systems for industrial agriculture, genetic engineering is an option. For example, the use of genetic engineering would allow a heterogeneous combination of cloned resistance genes to be peppered into a homogeneous varietal background. Such a multiline strategy would maintain desired performance and economically valuable product characteristics but would provide a diversity of resistance characteristics that are essential to the stable management of biotic stresses. In essence, this approach simulates the achievement of early farmers who created heterogeneous landrace varieties that were characterized by uniform expression of specific characteristics. Cultural practices that involve the simultaneous or sequential planting of transgenic multilines containing different resistance genes along with nontransgenic plants of the same variety would promote diversity both within a field and over time.

A variety of different strategies for engineering resistance are currently available, including the use of *Bt* (McGaughey, Gould, and Gelernter 1998*)*, *Pht*

(Bowen et al. 2000*)*, viral coat-protein, movement protein, chitinase, proteinase inhibitors, and others. Any of these could be used in combination with different plant promoters to diversify the timing, amount, and type of resistance that was being expressed at any point in space or time.

Using genetic engineering, plant breeders have access to one of the few available mechanisms for efficiently generating crop varieties that present a genetically diverse face to pests and pathogens while simultaneously providing a uniform, high-quality edible food or fiber product for consumption. Such a system would avoid imposing excessive selection pressure on pest populations, and would thus minimize the risk of pest epidemics while meeting market demand. The next generation of genetically engineered crop varieties in the industrial world is likely to reflect these considerations. If appropriate economic incentives were put in place—including access to genes; promoters; transformation systems; and productive, cross-bred varieties as starting material—such creative applications of biotechnology could simultaneously augment the genetic diversity of crop varieties and enhance ecological stability in both the developed and developing world.

Can Agricultural Biotechnology Strengthen Efforts to Protect Genetic Diversity?

One of the specters of modern agriculture is that it represents a vast movement toward uniformity. This has profound ecological and dietary implications for all people. An important feature of industrial agriculture was altering the environment in an effort to optimize conditions for crop production. In the process, the diversity inherent in our agricultural production systems followed a declining curve as fewer and fewer species were planted over larger and larger areas, and variety development and seed production were increasingly consolidated in a few, large multinational corporations. Wild flora and fauna have been increasingly threatened as human populations continue to expand and industrial agricultural systems are pushed to the limit in an effort to maximize global food production. It has been eloquently argued that the high productivity of industrial agriculture and the application of new techniques aimed at making it more efficient, including biotechnology, serve to protect wild lands that would have been converted to farmland had the system been less productive (Swaminathan 2000; Trewavas 2001). Yet, throughout the world, people are also questioning the methods, technologies, and philosophies underlying the current food-production system. In these discussions, it is often assumed that the use of biotechnology in food production will inevitably lead to further ecological disruption and economic disparity without directly benefiting consumers.

I would challenge this perspective. There are many forms of biotechnology and many ways in which it could be used to augment productivity while benefiting consumers and the environment. My own research has been able to demonstrate that wild relatives of crop species can harbor favorable genes that are not expressed in the phenotype of the parent (Tanksley and McCouch 1997). For example, genes that enhance the yield characteristics of cultivated rice can be introgressed from low-yielding, wild relatives using traditional crossing and selection coupled with the use of molecular maps and markers. This use of biotechnology enables simultaneous identification of regions of the genome containing unexpectedly favorable alleles and more efficient generation of improved varieties. While this is accomplished without the use of genetic engineering, identifying the genes underlying the traits of interest provides information about the DNA sequence of those genes, which in turn can be used as the basis for identifying novel variation in additional wild and exotic germ plasm. This use of knowledge derived from biotechnology provides a strong case for preserving wild species because of the direct and far-reaching value their germ plasm may bring to future plant improvement efforts. Nature offers an invaluable window on the array of unexpected and unpredictable biological solutions that work in the "real world," and modern biotechnology offers tools to understand, mechanistically, how and why things work. The tools of biotechnology make it possible to identify evolutionarily conserved genes or biochemical pathways in distantly related organisms and to identify the common molecular basis of these mechanisms so that the information derived from attention to these diverse biological systems can be used to generate new solutions. By increasing appreciation of the knowledge that can be derived from studying all forms of genetic variation that have withstood the test of evolutionary time in nature, biotechnology argues strongly in favor of continued efforts to protect and conserve both wild and domesticated forms of biodiversity.

Can Future Technical Advances Be Expected to Provide Solutions to Current Concerns?

Some of the most exciting technical advances in biotechnology involve the ability to generate novel forms of genetic variation by shuffling the genome from within rather than by exchanging segments of DNA between organisms. Ever since Barbara McClintock discovered transposable elements and postulated their role in evolution, scientists have been fascinated with the idea that these elements might be harnessed to drive an accelerated form of evolution from which new genotypes could be selected. By recognizing that organisms harbor mechanisms that can be activated to dramatically alter the structure and function of their genomes, investigating the possibility of using those mechanisms to drive genetic change without crossing species barriers becomes increasingly interesting. While these approaches have only recently begun to generate commercial products, they offer new opportunities for using the natural potential of living things to generate variation. This may be a direction that is more acceptable to the public than current efforts to move genes from one organism to another. The key is that abundant genetic variation can be generated through internal gene shuffling and recombination (Stemmer 1994; Crameri and Stemmer 1995). Developing efficient approaches to the selection of useful material from such a process requires technical innovation and deciding which problems merit attention and would benefit from a more participatory approach than is commonly used today.

As a major research activity, farmers, consumers, seed companies, life science corporations, independent scientists, representatives of government, consumer groups, and environmentalists from around the world could be brought directly into a global dialogue about what kinds of genetic improvements are most needed or justified in an agricultural context. Commitment to open-ended dialogue is the best way to forge new partnerships that will help shape the future of biotechnology in agriculture. Partnerships between the public and private sectors could begin to address many of the opportunities for applying biotechnology to benefit the world's poor. It is unrealistic to expect the private sector to pursue goals on its own that have no realistic expectation of economic return. It is equally unrealistic to expect the public sector to find solutions to the problems of feeding the human population in the 21st century unless there is a sizeable investment in public research in both developed and developing countries.

What is needed to catalyze a collective response to the problem of feeding the world in the years ahead? Suggested solutions include freer licensing of key technologies or materials for use in developing countries where markets do not compete with the interests of corporate owners (Conway and Toenniessen 1999; Gonsalves 1998; James 1998; Rivera-Bustamante 1995; Wambugu 1999), and establishment of well-formulated biosafety regulations and the ability to evaluate transgenic material in carefully controlled field trials in countries anxious to receive transgenic test material (James 1998; Duvick 1999; Herrera-Estrella 1999). The benefits or risks of adopting transgenic varieties need to be evaluated on a case-by-case basis by trained biological and social scientists from the countries concerned. This requires the creation of new opportunities for scientists from both developed and developing countries in both the public and private sectors to work together to find solutions for problems that will determine who the world feeds in the 21st century.

Conclusion

To achieve a more productive and sustainable agricultural production system and a more equitable distribution of goods and services in the years ahead, we humans must nurture both our innate creativity and our deepest sense of ethical and moral connections to each other and to the earth. We must ensure that we are all as well-informed as possible in the technical, social, economic, and ethical realms so that our considerations of the future are not limited by the perspectives and accomplishments of today. We must incorporate an understanding of how we grow and develop as a species so that we can evolve a visionary concept of who we are and how we will live together. In doing so, it is imperative that people seek to maintain an awareness of and respect for the diversity of human situations and the diversity of possible solutions to the problems we face collectively. Clearly, not all people have the same choices nor will they express the same preferences even if given the same choices. Careful consideration and creative exploration of different options for food production and distribution systems and of the risks and benefits that different systems present to different groups of people are essential as we face the challenges ahead.

CHAPTER 4

Resources, Technology, and Public and Private Choices

KEITH WIEBE

M uch attention has been given in recent years to concerns about the ability of the world's natural resource base to support increasing demands for food and other agricultural products without irreversible damage to the environment. Pinstrup-Andersen and Pandya-Lorch note in Chapter 1 that over the next two decades, trends in population, income, and urbanization are projected to raise world demand for cereals, roots, and tubers by nearly 40 percent, and for meat by nearly 60 percent. Given land constraints in some areas and environmental concerns about agricultural land expansion in others, most of the increased production necessary to meet this demand will have to come from increased productivity on land already in agricultural production.

As noted by Lal and McCouch in Chapters 2 and 3, respectively, concerns have been expressed about the extent to which resource degradation affects agricultural productivity, and the extent to which technological innovation will be able to address such challenges. For example, a recent assessment concludes that nearly 40 percent of the world's agricultural land is seriously degraded, undermining both present and future productive capacity (IFPRI 2000). In the case of both land degradation and new technology, a critical but often underappreciated dimension of the challenge involves the degree to which markets and other institutions provide farmers with incentives to adopt resource management practices and technologies whose impacts are felt beyond the farm and into the future.

Recognizing this dimension is critical to understanding how resources and technology can be managed to improve food security, as well as to determining the nature and scale of appropriate policy responses.

Land Resources

Land—embodying soils, climate, and other characteristics—is one of the most basic resources used in agricultural production. Land resources and agricultural productivity affect food security both through their impact on food supply and through their impact on the incomes of that half of the world's people whose livelihoods depend directly on agriculture. About 11 percent of global land area is considered arable land (that is, land in temporary or permanent crops), ranging from 5 percent in the Middle East and North Africa to 43 percent in South Asia. Arable land per capita ranges from 0.1 hectare in East Asia and the Pacific to 0.7 hectares in the United States.

In recent decades, agricultural land area has increased at an average rate of 0.3 percent annually worldwide, and as rapidly as 1.3 percent annually in Latin America and the Caribbean. This increase often represents expansion of cultivation onto marginal lands, such as those with shallow soils or steep slopes. Permanent pasture has remained relatively constant in area, indicating that the majority of the net increase in cropland area has occurred ultimately at the expense of areas formerly under forest or woodland cover. On the basis of projected growth in cereal demand and yields, Rosegrant, Ringler, and Gerpacio (1999) argue that land conversion will slow in the next two decades, and that area constraints will not threaten global food supplies in the foreseeable future. On the basis of their assessment of agroecological zones, food needs, and technological development and adoption potential, Alexandratos and Bruinsma (1999) also conclude that projected increases in agricultural land area are only a small proportion of total unused land with potential for rainfed crop production. Others caution that land conversion continues at high levels in some regions, such as Sub-Saharan Africa, and raise concerns about future production constraints in those areas (Houghton 1994).

Even if the rate of land conversion for agriculture slows in the coming decades, land already used for agricultural production is also subject to increasingly intensive production. As explained by Lal in Chapter 2, in the absence of appropriate management practices, this can lead to degradation through nutrient depletion, soil erosion, and other processes. Using data from the global assessment of land degradation by Oldeman, Hakkeling, and Sombroek (1991), combined with estimates of productivity losses generated by Dregne and Chou (1992), Crosson (1997b) argues that erosion-induced, on-site productivity losses are actually quite low on a global scale, averaging 0.1 to 0.2 percent per year. This is approximately one-tenth of the rate of annual average yield growth in recent decades (see Chapter 1). These rates are not trivial, but they also are not cause for undue alarm, keeping in mind that food insecurity is more a problem of individual and household access to food—whether through local production or purchase—than of global food availability.

Of greater concern than global average yield losses, for food production and income generation as well as for environmental reasons, are the impacts of soil degradation in specific areas. Recent reviews indicate that land degradation can have significant on- and off-site impacts on income and environmental quality in many areas, even if it does not threaten global food supply (Scherr 1999; Pagiola 1999). Scherr and Yadav (1996) identify a number of such "hot spots" where various forms of land degradation pose a significant threat, including nutrient depletion in parts of Africa, salinization in irrigated areas of Asia and the Middle East, and erosion on hillsides in Latin America. On the basis of the global assessment by Oldeman, Hakkeling, and Sombroek (1991), they report that degradation of agricultural land and permanent pasture is most extensive in Africa (65 percent and 31 percent, respectively), while degradation of forest and woodland is most extensive in Asia (27 percent). Bumb and Baanante (1996) report that in many countries of Sub-Saharan Africa, soil nutrients are removed at rates three to four times those of nutrient replenishment, while Lal (1995) estimates that soil erosion has reduced crop yields in Sub-Saharan Africa, relative to what they would have been otherwise, by about 6 percent.

Estimates of the global extent and severity of land degradation, and of its productivity impacts, are based on expert opinion, extrapolation from site-specific studies, or both. As Lal (1998) points out, these estimates are subject to numerous uncertainties and need to be treated with considerable caution. Improvements in both approaches are possible through recent advances in geographic information systems and data on soils, climate, and land cover.

Taking advantage of such advances, research by Wiebe et al. (2000) builds on earlier studies of agricultural productivity by using spatially referenced soil and climate data combined with high-resolution land-cover data to create improved indicators of resource quality. Econometric analysis of these data, along with data on agricultural inputs and outputs from 110 countries for the period 1961–97, shows that international differences in resource quality contribute significantly to observed differences in agricultural labor productivity, above and beyond the effect of indicators used in earlier studies. Better soils and climate are associated with increases of 20 percent or more in agricultural output per worker in most regions, everything else being equal.

More important, improved estimates of land quality's effects on agricultural output per worker also improve estimation of the effects of other conventional and nonconventional factors on productivity. The results of Wiebe et al. (2000) suggest a hierarchy of constraints related to land quality exists that limits agricultural productivity in developing countries. In countries poorly endowed with soils and climate, basic inputs—such as fertilizer, water (in the form of irrigation), and institutional stability—are more important than they are in countries that are relatively well endowed in terms of soil and climate. Only when these constraints have been overcome do factors such as labor quality, road density, and mechanization become significantly associated with improvements in agricultural productivity—as they are in countries with better soils and climate.

These findings with regard to the productivity impacts of differences in land quality are inherently cross-sectional thus far. Nevertheless, they also suggest the potential productivity impact of changes in land quality over time—for example, through investment in improved soil fertility or, conversely, through land degradation. In a recent analysis, den Biggelaar et al. (2001) combined spatially referenced data on soil-specific erosion rates and observed crop yield impacts from 90 original field studies to estimate erosion-induced losses in production for maize, wheat, soybeans, and cotton in North America. Annual yield losses varied by a factor of 10 in percentage terms, from 0.03 percent per year for wheat on alfisols in the United States to 0.27 percent per year for soybeans on ultisols in the United States. Preliminary analysis suggests an even greater range of impacts internationally.

Technology

As Susan McCouch points out in Chapter 3, humans have used artificial selection to modify plants and animals for desirable traits for some 10,000 years. The pace of technological innovation increased rapidly over the course of the 20th century, corresponding to a shift in the definition of biotechnology from genetic modification in general to new knowledge about natural processes and genetic manipulation at the DNA level. The impact of such innovation is clear in the doubling of average cereal yields in developing countries over the past three decades: yield gains account for nearly 90 percent of cereal production growth in developing countries since the beginning of the Green Revolution, and about half of yield gains are attributable to genetic improvements (Byerlee, Heisey, and Pingali 1999).

McCouch also points out that the concerns of the world's poor farmers and consumers are much different than those of the world's wealthy, and much less likely to be heard. As a result, appropriate incentives and responsible use are necessary to address these concerns and achieve the full potential of biotechnology.

It is critically important to recognize the differences that exist in incentives for developing various technologies, such as drought-tolerant maize or golden rice as opposed to herbicide-tolerant soybeans, and that those differences have important implications for public and private research agendas. It is these sorts of distinctions that deserve further attention with regard to both soil degradation and biotechnology.

Private Choices and Public Impacts

Both soil conservation and biotechnology have potentially significant impacts on food security and the global environment. The impacts that soil conservation and biotechnology actually have on food security and the environment depend critically on decisions made by the users of those technologies, that is, farmers. Markets generally provide farmers with incentives to address issues involving immediate or short-term impacts on their own fields. For example, farmers are likely to adopt conservation practices or pest-resistant crop varieties when the cost to them of such practices is outweighed by the benefits to them in terms of productivity gains (or losses avoided). In the absence of appropriate policy measures, markets typically provide weaker incentives to address issues involving impacts farther in the future, such as future productivity losses. In addition, markets often provide farmers with little (if any) incentive to address issues involving impacts that occur at a distance, such as downstream sedimentation or loss of genetic diversity.

This point can be illustrated by graphing some of the issues raised about soil degradation and biotechnology in terms of their impacts in two dimensions, with the horizontal dimension representing time and the vertical dimension representing space, that is, distance from the point at which decisions are made about the use of a particular technology. (A similar graph was used in a different context by Knox, Meinzen-Dick, and Hazell 1999.)

Soil degradation, for example, may reduce yields on a farmer's fields in the relatively short term, and evidence indicates that he or she will generally take steps to mitigate that effect (Figure 4.1). Some forms of soil degradation—such as nutrient depletion—can generally be feasibly reversed given current technologies and market conditions, but others—such as topsoil loss due to erosion—are effectively irreversible. Soil degradation may also reduce yields over the longer term, and again evidence indicates that farmers will generally take steps to address this decline if they are confident that they will be able to realize the future benefits of investments made today.

How soils are actually managed to avoid, minimize, or reverse degradation depends on a variety of factors influencing farmer decisions, including the prices

Figure 4.1 Dimensions of soil degradation impacts

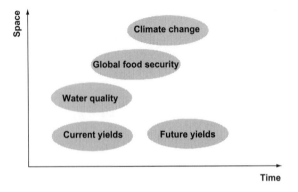

of agricultural inputs and outputs, farmer characteristics, and land tenure (Soule, Tegene, and Wiebe 2000). Where markets function well and property rights are well defined, farmers generally have an incentive to manage soils to protect their long-term productive potential (Hopkins et al. 1998). Where land tenure is uncertain or access to credit is limited, on the other hand, this incentive may be weak and farmers may not find it optimal to adopt costly soil conservation measures (Pagiola 1999).

In addition to its effects on productivity, soil degradation may also have important economic and environmental effects beyond the farmer's field, including effects on water quality, global food security, and climate change (Lal this volume; Crosson 1995). Since these impacts are felt off-site, farmers typically do not have incentives to spend their own resources to address these effects sufficiently to meet society's objectives, and generally need additional incentives to address such concerns sufficiently. These concerns motivate policy measures to encourage increased adoption of conservation measures by farmers in many countries.

Issues related to biotechnology can also be considered in this framework (Figure 4.2). From the farmer's perspective, various technologies have the potential to reduce the use of inputs (such as pesticides), improve the quality and quantity of outputs (such as micronutrient content and reduced losses to pests or spoilage), and thus increase income. If the on-farm benefits of such technologies are perceived to outweigh the costs of adoption, farmers have an incentive to use them.

As McCouch points out in Chapter 3, these technologies may also generate impacts off the farm and into the future. These include impacts on consumption, the environment, and food quality (including human health), and may be both positive and negative in terms of meeting society's objectives. As with the

Figure 4.2 Dimensions of biotechnology impacts

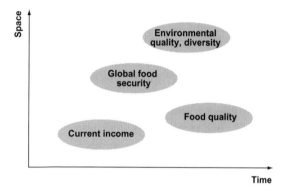

off-site effects of soil degradation, farmers typically do not have incentives to spend their own resources to address these broader effects sufficiently to meet society's objectives. Furthermore, society's concerns about the potential negative impacts of biotechnology, particularly about genetic engineering, will in turn influence farmers' expectations about the returns to those technologies. It is significant to note that, while farmers represent a small percentage of the population in the developed countries, more than half of the people in developing countries earn their livelihoods through agriculture, and are thus potentially involved in making these calculations.

One point that bears emphasis is that the positioning of these issues on these axes is strictly relative and approximate. Furthermore, it is important to keep in mind that each of the items is located with reference to its approximate distance in space and time from the decisionmaker, and implies no assessment of its relative magnitude or importance. Nevertheless such a perspective, even in general terms, highlights the importance of recognizing that the public research needs and policy challenges associated with these issues are distinct from private priorities, and this distinction relates directly to the question of *who* the world will feed, as opposed to whether the world can produce enough food.

Implications for Incentives and Institutions

Improving understanding of the relationship between sustainable resource use and global food security requires recognition of the reality that global food and resource-related processes are driven ultimately by the choices made by individual decisionmakers who clear land, draw water, plant crops, and raise livestock to meet their own goals. These choices are influenced in turn by the ways in which property rights and institutional systems structure markets to balance the interests of individual decisionmakers with those of the public, both locally and globally, and both in the short term and over the longer term.

Without stable institutions, markets are unlikely to offer sufficient incentives for investment in the productive and sustainable use of natural and other resources. It is notable that per capita food production has increased for the world as a whole and in most regions in recent decades, but has fallen in two relatively land abundant but institutionally turbulent regions: Sub-Saharan Africa and the countries of the former Soviet Union (World Bank 1998).

Without appropriate institutions, markets are also unlikely to offer incentives for the protection of resources for which property rights may be imperfectly defined or enforced—whether on a local scale, such as grazing lands traditionally managed under a common-property regime that has subsequently disintegrated; or on a global scale, such as the earth's atmosphere (Dasgupta and Mäler 1994; Wiebe and Meinzen-Dick 1998). Where tenure systems are absent or have ceased to function properly, development of well-defined and carefully enforced institutional arrangements will be necessary (but not sufficient) for sustainable resource use.

Finally, the efficiency with which resources are used to meet food-security and environmental goals over the long term will depend not only on the performance of markets and other institutions but also on improvements in productivity, on the protection and appropriate use of genetic diversity, and on other dimensions of the global agricultural economy that are addressed elsewhere in this volume.

The general point that deserves emphasis in each of these cases is that, while new technologies offer considerable potential for improving environmental quality and food security, actual outcomes will depend critically on the incentives faced by the various individuals and institutions involved. The greater the spatial scale of potential costs and benefits, and the farther they are into the future, the greater is the challenge for policymakers to structure appropriate incentives and institutions, and the greater is the importance of research and improved understanding of the alternatives available.

PART III

Ensuring Access to Food

CHAPTER 5

The Critical Role of Income Constraints

G. EDWARD SCHUH

In thinking about ways to alleviate food insecurity, there is a tendency to emphasize new production technology for staple food crops. Such technology is certainly important in increasing food supplies and in promoting economic growth generally, especially in the low-income developing countries. However, the role of the social sciences is also critical. In particular, it is necessary to better understand the economic policies needed to promote economic growth and development, the nature of opportunities and constraints facing food-insecure households, and the importance of safety nets to protect the most vulnerable members of society.

Three important sources help to frame the challenge. Pinstrup-Andersen and Pandya-Lorch (Chapter 1) provide a starting point by documenting the dimensions of the current food-insecurity problem around the world. Amartya Sen (1981) made the important point that poverty, not lack of food supplies per se, is the fundamental cause of malnutrition and hunger. In addition, the World Bank's 1986 policy paper on food security criticized the distortions in economic policy that were commonly used to ensure a cheap food supply as the means of dealing with food insecurity, provided additional evidence on the importance of poverty alleviation as the means of achieving food security, and stressed the importance of economic growth and safety nets as means to alleviate poverty.

Pinstrup-Andersen and Pandya-Lorch note that the total *number* of food-insecure people worldwide has declined from 960 million people in 1969–71 to 791 million in 1995–97, a significant accomplishment. The largest reduction has taken place in East and Southeast Asia, where economic growth has been the most pervasive and most vigorous during this period. More modest reductions have occurred in South Asia and North Africa. However, the number of food-insecure people has doubled during this period in Sub-Saharan Africa, where economic growth has been stagnant. It is worth noting that food insecurity is a problem even in the United States, as discussed in the 1999 *United States Action Plan on Food Security* (Interagency Working Group on Food Security and the Food Security Advisory Committee of the Board for International Food and Agricultural Development 1999).

In relative terms, progress in reducing the food-insecurity problem over time has been significant. The *share* of the world's population that was food insecure declined from 37 percent in 1969–71 to 18 percent in the most recent period. That reduction is testimony to the pace of agricultural modernization that has taken place during this period, to the pace and pervasiveness of economic growth, and to the increased integration of the global economy.

This chapter focuses on the ways in which income constraints may be overcome and, in particular, on how contributions from science must interface with social, economic, and institutional change, and with commitments by governments to improving food access and achieving the desired outcome of food security for all. This chapter is divided into three parts:

- the contributions of macroeconomic policy, especially international trade policy and its interactions with development policy as the means of promoting *global* economic growth;

- the importance of the household in addressing the poverty problem and the need for both policymakers and scientists to give more attention to that important institution in society as the means to alleviate poverty and promote economic growth; and

- the role of safety nets and how they might be supported.

Macroeconomic Policy

INTERNATIONAL TRADE

To promote economic growth, it is essential to create an economic environment that is stable and that provides appropriate incentives to producers. However, the role of international trade in promoting economic growth and alleviating poverty is also important, especially in light of the concerns voiced over the past year regarding globalization and the World Trade Organization.

Such concerns appear to be two-fold. The first is the concern about low wages in developing countries and fears that competition from other countries could lead to unemployment in the domestic economy. Much of that fear seems to be misplaced, after 10 years of uninterrupted expansion in the U.S. economy and levels of unemployment at the lowest levels in 30 years. It is important to keep in mind that low wages do not necessarily correspond to low-cost output. Rather, productivity is the key issue. As Wassily Leontief noted some years ago, the United States tends to export labor-intensive goods and services despite relatively high wages, and does so in large part because of the high productivity of the U.S. labor force (Leontief 1953).

The other concern relates to the basic principle of comparative advantage, which is a relative, rather than an absolute, concept. Countries have to export in order to import, and to focus on only one side of the exchange is a mistake. In fact, much of the recent sustained economic growth in the U.S. economy has been driven in large part by international trade. Even imports can facilitate economic growth if they provide modern inputs and raw material for the domestic production sectors.

A quiet revolution has been taking place in economics that provides some important insights on this issue. The centerpiece of this revolution is what is described as "induced growth models," which have shifted the focus of traditional growth models away from their emphasis on growth accounting in an *ex post* sense to an emphasis on the forces that induce economic growth. The new perspective provides for the first time a link between international trade theory and policy on the one hand and economic growth and growth policy on the other. The link comes from revitalizing the ideas of Adam Smith, who published his book on *The Wealth of Nations* in 1776, and Allyn Young, who wrote in 1929 about sectoral specialization as a source of external economies in generating economic growth and development.

Adam Smith put a great deal of emphasis on specialization and the division of labor as viewed at the microeconomic level. He argued that this specialization and division of labor was an important source of economic growth and the elevation of per capita incomes. He wrote, of course, at a time in which production technology did not have the improvements it does today. Smith also emphasized that economic growth driven by this means was limited by the extent of the market. That meant that the size of an economy eventually put a constraint on economic growth.

Allyn Young revitalized Smith's perspectives on specialization and division of labor, and gave them a new interpretation. He argued that the specialization and division of labor also took place at the sectoral level as activities required for the production of a single product, say an automobile, were spun off as separate sectors of the economy. That specialization and division of labor also was, in his view, an important source of economic growth. In the case of the automobile, the production of wheels, tires, parts, and even metals could be done at a lower cost if done in specialized economic sectors. In some cases, these economies could be widespread.

The important contribution of this insight is that national limits to the growth process are overcome in the context of open international trade. Rather than being limited by the size of the domestic economy, a nation's growth process could be unlimited as long as the nation was willing to specialize and engage in international trade. Thus, the size of the domestic economy no longer was important so long as the conditions identified were present. This is an enormously uplifting idea, and one of great value to small countries, or to those who in the past have pursued autarchic economic policies.

The success of the rapidly growing economies of Asia, before their late-1990s crises in foreign exchange markets, is largely attributed to this kind of specialization, with the key being to identify niches in the international markets and take advantage of them. Notably, it is in Asia, and in the newly industrializing countries, that food insecurity has been reduced the most since the end of the 1960s. Moreover, the driving force behind economic development and improved food security in those economies was not in increasing their food supplies, but in generating economic growth through expanded exports of manufactured products.

The contribution of international trade goes beyond this specialization and division of labor. International trade also provides competition to the domestic economy that leads to modernization and a search for efficiency in resource use and allocation. It also can be an important source of new production technology. Finally, an open economy with sound trade and other economic policies becomes an attractive source of investment by the international economy. Thus, savings may be mobilized from other parts of the world to help finance a higher rate of economic development and growth.

The policy implications from more careful reflection on international trade are clear. First, countries should move to an increasingly open international trade policy so they benefit from the increased specialization and division of labor. Second, they need to invest in the science and technology that will make them more competitive in the international economy. Finally, countries need to maintain proper adjustment policies to help those individuals and households that are dislocated by international trade adjust to new opportunities. (This final implication will be discussed further in subsequent sections.)

AGRICULTURAL RESEARCH AND POVERTY ALLEVIATION

Agricultural research and the development of new production technologies contribute to poverty alleviation in two important ways. First, when they focus on food staples, the new technologies will, through general-equilibrium effects in the economy as a whole, generally lead to lower prices for the commodities in question. Those lower prices are equivalent to increases in real income for consumers of those commodities. If the staples are widely consumed, the increases in per capita incomes will be widespread in the economy. Although the increase may be small for an individual household, the aggregate increase across the economy as a whole will be large. That is one of the reasons why the social rate of return to agricultural research is so high.

The more important issue is the relative benefit to the poor within society because they tend to spend a larger share of their income on food. This share may be as high as 70 to 80 percent in many cases. Thus, the benefits of investing in agricultural research should be considered in the context of the larger economy, recognizing impacts on consumers as well as on agricultural producers. A large share of the benefits may in fact go to the poor in urban areas.

Many observers argue that, to alleviate poverty, agricultural research should be focused on the problems of smallholders. In fact, this emphasis is so great now that general agricultural research programs around the world are being significantly distorted from paths that would contribute more widely to poverty alleviation if they were to concentrate on broader issues. With this emphasis on smallholders, insufficient recognition is given to an important feature of economic growth and development: large amounts of labor will inevitably have to leave agriculture, and most of that labor will come from the population of smallholders. Public resources might better be invested in education and training programs that would facilitate that shift.

Agricultural research can also contribute more generally to poverty alleviation if some part of it is directed to export or cash crops, or to crops that compete with imports. For example, foreign exchange will be earned from exports by making the agricultural sector more competitive in the international economy. In the case of crops that compete with imports, foreign exchange will be saved. In both cases, the increased supply of foreign exchange can be used to service foreign debt, or to finance higher rates of economic growth by making it possible to import critical imports of intermediate capital inputs and raw materials. If the increase in exchange earnings or savings is large enough, the value of the nation's currency in foreign exchange markets may actually rise.

It should be noted that export crops tend to be labor intensive, so increased competitiveness in this area would lead to direct increases in agricultural employment. By financing a higher rate of economic growth, agricultural research may also make it possible to generate additional employment through the expansion of the nonfarm sector. That would create employment opportunities for the poor who are leaving agriculture and contribute to poverty alleviation. If the increases in foreign exchange are sufficiently large to contribute to a rise in the value of the nation's currency, the benefits to society would be even more widespread.

The Importance of the Household

When policymakers and members of the international development community design policies to promote economic growth, they tend to think about the firm as the basis of their policies. In today's world they tend to think about policies to free up markets, or policy reform; stabilization policies to reduce inflation and stabilize foreign exchange markets; and subsidies in the form of cheap credit, privileged access to foreign exchange, or other direct subsidies to private or public firms. All of these policies—except for the last set—are necessary conditions for promoting economic growth. However, they are not, alone, *sufficient* conditions for promoting economic growth.

In addition to creating the right economic environment, public investments are also needed to promote economic growth and development. Critical public investments in this context include investments in physical infrastructure, investments in science and technology (including, especially in developing countries, investments in agricultural research), and investments in education and health. These are important sources of economic growth, with important implications for household welfare, and for the most part they are investments the private sector is not going to make—at least not at socially optimal levels.

A vibrant and vigorous private sector is obviously necessary if an economy is going to grow. However, the household is the key to alleviating the constraints to economic growth, and especially to reducing poverty in the economy. The household is important because most of the human capital in a society is produced there. Investments in human capital are inexpensive sources of economic growth, especially in the sense that they yield a high social rate of return. Moreover, in modern economies such as the United States', human capital is the source of almost all of the increases in per capita incomes and economic growth.

What forms do human capital take? From a household perspective, the list includes the nutrition, health, and education of both the children and the adults in the household, as well as the level of technology used in the household. The perspective of the new household economics teaches that the household must be thought of as a firm that acquires inputs from the market economy and combines them with household labor to produce goods and services. The failure of economists in general to recognize the importance of the household has caused them to neglect the fact that much of the important human capital in an economy is produced in the household.

This proposition about the role of the household is seen in its most obvious form, perhaps, in the cases of nutrition and health—important forms of human capital that are critical to both the physical and cognitive abilities of members of the household. The household may purchase food from the market, but that food is combined with labor in the household and converted into meals and adequate nutrition. The same applies to health more generally. Health care may be acquired from public-health posts or from private doctors. However, much of the production of sound health comes from the daily care and nurturing of the members of the household. This includes adequate nutrition, hygiene, and care and sustenance when one is ill.

Less widely recognized is the education and training that takes place in the household. Adults and older children are typically in a position to be teaching and developing cognitive and vocational skills on an almost continuous basis. Moreover, if members of the family are literate, much of their reading and self-study may take place within the household. Education and training are critical to raising the productivity of labor on farms, to gaining productive nonfarm employment, and even to raising the productivity of labor within the household.

Even more neglected is the role of the production technology used in the household. The sight of women and children carrying water and firewood on their heads for household use is common in the low-income developing countries. However, less commonly recognized is the fact that improvements in the form of new technology imbedded in public water systems, or improved stoves that use fuels other than firewood, could alleviate labor constraints in the household and raise the output of the household, especially in the production of human capital.

Finally, there is the critical role of the woman in the household. In rural areas of developing countries, the woman typically is the one mainly responsible for the production of the various forms of human capital identified above. However, she also contributes labor and often managerial inputs to farm production, and in many cases she is the main source of family labor for the production unit, especially when male members of the household are off working in nonfarm employment. Even when the household moves to urban areas, the woman still may be responsible for the household, even if she has gainful employment outside the household. Sadly, the importance of the woman in these multiple roles still continues to be neglected. Somewhat ironically, even when the importance of the woman in farm production and management is recognized, the response is often limited to providing a female extension agent to teach the woman improved farming skills, but nothing about how to better manage the household.

What policies are available to alleviate these constraints within the household? A starting place would be to emphasize the importance of literacy, formal schooling, and vocational training for women and girls. Improvements are being made on this front in many countries. However, there is still a long way to grow.

A second thrust should include an expanded research program to understand the widely differing social and economic conditions in households around the world. Although the family is the key social unit in almost every country in the world, knowledge of the economics of the household unit is still dramatically limited. A basic knowledge gap involves information on how time is used by all members in the household. Proper policies cannot be designed until these issues are better understood.

A related point is that research is needed to develop new process and product technology for the household. Unfortunately, many of us from developed economies, where women have made large advances in gaining employment in labor markets and ultimately economic independence, fail to recognize the role that household technology makes in reducing the demands on the time of the woman in the household, thus freeing her to participate in the labor market. Examples of improved product technology are legion, enabling time savings in common household chores. Less often recognized are women's other skills such as preparing nutritious meals, making efficient use of their time, and imparting knowledge to their children in their day-to-day interactions.

Finally, it is essential to recognize the importance of extension and adult education programs for women in poor households. These programs should not focus just on imparting farming skills, but also on teaching the women how to better manage their activities in the household. In a paper (2000) I originally gave at the CGIAR's poverty conference in Costa Rica, I called attention to the way extension programs began in the United States. The county extension office was typically staffed with a male extension agent who worked with the farmer and a female home demonstration agent who worked with the woman in the household. These home demonstration agents taught women nutrition and how to obtain it; health care and hygiene; and how to make more efficient use of time in the household. Nothing less than this, *plus* agricultural extension, is needed for the women in poor households of low-income countries.

Safety Nets

Even if policymakers follow all of the precepts described, the development process will bypass some individuals and households—some for short periods of time and others permanently. For that reason, safety nets of some kind or another are needed if food security for all is to be realized.

The labor-adjustment policies referred to above are one such safety net. The goal should be to retrain workers for alternative employment, and to help them relocate to alternative employment. As a corollary, some means of sustaining them through the training program and the process of relocation is often needed. Labor-intensive public works or food-for-work programs are examples of safety nets that have been important in providing both food and employment in times of economic distress in a wide variety of contexts. If properly designed—for example, to encourage self-targeting—these programs provide both a safety net to those most in need and an opportunity for developing economies to invest in the construction or maintenance of productive capital. It should be noted that facilitating labor mobility in this way also accelerates the rate of economic growth and development.

The problem of adjustment policies became controversial during the widespread economic reforms promoted by the World Bank and the International Monetary Fund during the 1980s and 1990s. In that case, these international institutions were trying to facilitate the large reforms in economic policy made necessary as a consequence of the international economic and debt crisis of that period. Those policies could have been easier to undertake by local policymakers, with less harm to the poor (who ultimately bore much of the costs of adjustment), with more effective policies. Because of the large currency devaluations required as part of those reforms, much of the burden of adjustment resided on the urban poor. These victims of the process could have benefited from targeted feeding programs. Ironically, food aid was available during that period. A more human face could have been put on the adjustment policies if more use had been made of food aid in the form of targeted feeding programs, rather than the widespread monetization of that food aid that occurred.

One way to address the issue of the workers who are permanently bypassed by the development process, or who are disabled in such a way that they cannot participate in the labor market or sustain themselves, is targeted feeding programs. These can be programs similar to the food-stamp program in the United States; specialized stores for the disadvantaged, as used in a number of countries; or other means of providing access to food. An important point of the World Bank's 1986 food-security paper, however, was that policies that generally distort the prices of food as the means to benefit the poor, tend to benefit the well-to-do the most and are counterproductive.

Concluding Comments

In thinking about alleviating the food-insecurity problem, the tendency is to put the emphasis on new production technology for food staples. Such technology is certainly important in promoting economic growth generally, especially in the low-income developing countries. However, as has been shown, the role of the social sciences is also critical. The economic policies required to promote economic growth and development need to be better understood, as does the household. Ways of protecting those who fail to benefit from the broader process of growth and development are also needed.

Alleviating the income constraints that lead to food insecurity must ultimately be based on a multipronged approach. In most countries, the modernization of agriculture to induce lower food prices and the reform of trade and exchange rate policy are critical as beginning points. However, an improved focus on the household in development policy is equally important, even though the benefits may take longer to realize. Finally, appropriate safety nets are needed for groups that are passed by the development process.

CHAPTER 6

Food from Peace and Roles of Women

ELLEN MESSER

In Chapter 1, Pinstrup-Andersen and Pandya-Lorch use demographic and production models to project the numbers and regional distribution of food-insecure people in 2020. They simultaneously consider the ways scientists (or the world) might address them. Subsequent chapters of this volume stress the importance of appropriate resource management and biotechnology. Overall, these scenarios suggest a more positive aggregate world food outlook than existed five years ago (Pinstrup-Andersen and Pandya-Lorch 1994), and indicate how governments, nongovernmental organizations (NGOs), and international agencies can reduce the numbers of undernourished people in developing countries through improved education (especially for women), better access to clean water, and greater participation by communities.

Another way to approach this question, however, is to ask: "Who will be able to feed themselves in the 21st century?" This makes the future of hunger less a technical question, and more a question of human rights and capabilities. Will the global community achieve the United Nations' goal of a universal right to food in the 21st century? Who will be left out—and why? Can the scientific community do anything differently to enhance human capabilities and freedoms so that more individuals can choose lives they really value, including nutritionally adequate food?

In reframing the question this way, I draw on the perspectives of Nobel laureate Amartya Sen (especially Sen 1999) and of Food First (the nongovernmental Institute for Food and Development Policy). Both call attention to the root causes of hunger, not just poverty but the social structures of injustice and inequality underlying it, and call for policy commitments to enhance all human capabilities (Sen 1999; Lappe, Collins, and Rosset 1998). Both emphasize the violence associated with hunger, including civil conflict. Both insist that improvements in food security and human welfare can only occur through programs that effectively consider democracy along with development. In either view, eliminating half the world's hunger by the United Nations' target year of 2015 (FAO 1999b) will require more than state-of-the-art analysis that is demographic, economic, and agricultural; enhanced soil management; biotechnology; and revitalized investments in nutrition, food, and agriculture. It will also require genuine commitment to human rights, related transformations in agricultural and development policies, and greater participation by local peoples, demanding more appropriate actions on the part of governments and international agencies.

Two particularly important facets of a genuine commitment to human rights in this context are distinct but related efforts to create a more secure and peaceful world and to ensure equal opportunity for women. Peace and full participation of women, either singly or in combination, have the potential to substantively change projected outcomes for food security in the 21st century.[1] The following two sections consider what peace might contribute to future food supply and demand, particularly in Sub-Saharan Africa; and what might be gained from a woman-centered approach to food and nutrition planning, from agricultural research and extension to more efficient processing and consumption. A final section connects these two factors to additional institutional perspectives raised in other discussions in this volume.

Food from Peace

Armed conflicts (involving more than 1,000 deaths) constitute a significant cause of deteriorating food scenarios in developing countries and have been shown to be salient factors in the famines of the 1980s and 1990s. Recent research (Messer, Cohen, and D'Costa 1998) shows that populations in 47 countries suffered food insecurity as a consequence of food wars, a concept that includes both the use of hunger as a weapon in active conflict and the food insecurity that accompanies and follows as a consequence, because prolonged conflicts destroy land, waterworks, markets, infrastructure, and human communities. Historically, conflict and food insecurity are linked in a destructive cycle, where a principal source of conflict lies in lack of food security, which creates new potential for conflict. From this it follows that food security can help prevent conflict and is essential for sustained and peaceful recovery after wars have ended.

This research (Messer, Cohen, and D'Costa 1998) also estimated the magnitude of food-production losses due to conflict by examining trends in war-torn countries of southern Africa. The authors first compared mean food production per capita with "peace-adjusted" values (which indicate what food production might have been in the absence of conflict in the region). In 13 of 14 countries studied, food production was lower in war years. Differences were as small as 3.4 percent in Kenya and as large as 44 percent in Angola, with a mean difference of 12.3 percent. The authors then calculated differences in mean food-production growth rates during war and nonwar years. This method adjusted annual growth figures to represent "food from peace" as a percentage of the production the region might have produced had peace prevailed. Reductions in food-production growth rates were observed in all countries except Nigeria and were cumulative: from 1.3 to 3.5 percent in the 1980s, and from 3.9 to 5.3 percent in the 1990s. Although the data are rough, the point is clear: to reduce food insecurity, Africa and other regions need peace.

Beyond the quantitative data, findings also indicated that development projects themselves can be a source of conflict, where would-be beneficiaries perceive unfairness in distribution of land, water, and goods and take action against perceived relative deprivation and injustice. These combined quantitative and qualitative findings have two important implications. First, the findings suggest that most countries and regions that are currently food insecure are not hopeless underproducers but are still experiencing the effects of past or present conflicts, political instability, and poor governance. Their food-production capacities are higher, and their food outlooks in the medium to longer term are brighter, than evident in most current projections. A key production variable in such cases is peace, although agricultural investment in improved seeds, more efficient land and water management, and projects to save and restore appropriate seeds are also very important.

Second, while agricultural investment can be an important deterrent to conflict, its actual relationship to civil strife is complex. Although a recent study commissioned by the NGO Future Harvest (De Soysa and Gleditsch 1999), which is related to the Consultative Group on International Agricultural Research (CGIAR), reached the simple conclusion that agricultural investment can help prevent conflict, it included a detailed Indian case study that demonstrates how complex the politics really are, and how successful outcomes depend on additional political factors that promote social justice. Agricultural investment can be carried out in ways that promote peace, but such development assistance needs to incorporate conflict prevention explicitly into policies, programs, and project planning, implementation, and evaluation. Case studies showing how aid that is sensitive to local participation can support peace rather than conflict have been produced for postconflict situations (Anderson 1999) but less often for conflict prevention. Experts designing programs of agricultural investment need to be aware of existing political circumstances in order to choose strategies that will foster cooperation among communities (or groups within communities). For example, provision of appropriate agricultural tools and seeds has been recognized as a critical step in the restoration of food production, food security, and peace during and immediately following periods of conflict (FAO 1998), and may contribute to conflict prevention as well.[2] However, programs need to be structured so that they allow active participation by women as well as men, particularly where the potential for conflict remains high. Researchers assessing connections between development assistance and conflict in Rwanda (Jefremovas 1991; Newbury 1992) have argued that women's capacities must be enhanced not only to increase food production, reduce food insecurity, and prevent nutritional insecurity, but also to help prevent conflict.

Women and Food

Women make up half of the world's population and more than half of the developing world's farming population.[3] A number of studies have found positive correlations between women's income and child nutritional status.[4] Evidence also indicates that female-headed households generally have lower income, in part because they have less access to productive resources, and also because child care and domestic chores leave women with less time to earn cash income.[5] Women's health and nutrition are special concerns, because women are often self-depriving or involuntarily deprived of food. Policymakers tend to characterize women as the "shock absorbers" of households, who absorb shortfalls in income or consumption, often at some nutritional cost to themselves (Quisumbing et al. 1995). In human terms, they often suffer abuse of the human right to adequate food and nutrition (ICN 1992); in economic terms, as a result of food deprivation they are less productive of goods and of household health. Their undernutrition also affects the nutritional status of the next generation because underweight women are more likely to give birth to infants with low birth weights.

Since the 1970s, there have been concerted efforts to involve women more centrally in development programs. These have included capacity-building programs to improve women's access to formal education and training, as well as specially targeted women's health and women-in-development programs designed to increase women's contributions to economic growth and other measures of human development. However, women still face discrimination and exclusion from above as well as horizontally (through gender-based discrimination in control of productive resources and income). Men are offered cash and field-crop programs; women are offered home vegetable gardens or cooking classes. Programs that claim to target women as beneficiaries often are not the same economic and production programs aimed toward men. Stereotypes of "women's agriculture" or "women's work" persist; distinguishing "women's work" makes women and their production visible and meaningful to economic planners (for example, Boserup 1965, 1970) but marginalizes women and their work from mainstream agricultural improvement plans. Agricultural investment programs that are separate, unequal, and gender specific also endure because of gender biases in science and development policy (for example, Downs, Kerner, and Reyna 1991).

Also constraining women's productivity are political and economic factors, including lack of ownership rights or direct access to land. Although women may gain use rights by custom and permission of male (owner) relatives, lack of secure tenure provides them with less incentive to invest in practices or crops (such as trees) that provide benefits only over the long term. They also have limited incentive to farm cash crops on lands they do not control, where products will accrue to male owners (even their husbands). Inequality and gender discrimination also mean women may lack access to water for irrigation or other purposes, technology, or new equipment.

Reversing agricultural underproduction by women will entail removing constraints as well as creating new opportunities. Equality before the law and secure access to land, water, and other factors of production are obvious steps, although they usually encounter resistance at all social levels. Even without major changes in the rules, women sometimes substantially improve production when they see market opportunities, as where Nigerian women, responding to urban market incentives, raised peri-urban production on land they did not own in unanticipated ways (Guyer 1998).

Food and nutritional security and sustainable management of local ecological systems are tightly tied to issues of gender and participation (Rhoades 1984). Food and agricultural planners have taken first steps toward participation by consulting individual farmers, or more rarely, whole communities, about agricultural intensification programs that are supposed to change their lives (Conway 1999). However, beyond the farmer-first viewpoint is the question of which farmers should be addressed, because women are often left out of the consultations, despite providing more than half of farm labor in Africa and substantial proportions in Asia and Latin America.

Women's access to information and materials is often restricted because there are few women extension agents, and even fewer women scientists in developing countries. The United Nations Environment Programme reported in 1988 that less than 1 percent of government-employed agricultural advisors in Asia and the Middle East were female, only 3 percent in Africa, and 8.5 percent in Latin America (Brown et al. 1995). For religious or other cultural reasons, male extension workers may work only with males and avoid contacts with females, and women may find it harder to find the time to meet with extension workers because of their duties as household keepers as well as farmers. Women may also lack the education, including fluency in the lingua franca, to converse with extension agents. All contribute to an impression that "women's agriculture" is inherently less productive than men's. However, given the same opportunities, information, and factors of production, females might well outperform males; they might also make different agricultural choices.

Removing the multiple barriers to women's access to extension requires deliberate steps, which may include training female extension workers, designing programs for mixed male-female farming groups, or transmitting information by media, such as radio. Lower educational levels may limit women's access to credit or their ability to use new scientific agricultural information. The less educated may be perceived to be less willing to adopt new cash crops, although the real problem may be that women grow subsistence crops for which no credit is provided and do not have access to the credit necessary to adopt other crops. NGOs in South Asia seek to provide innovative solutions to surmount these multiple systemic obstacles through systemwide programs that provide female-to-female extension, credit, education, and in some cases child care and maternal–child health services (Chen 1986).

Eliminating bias in access to education has longer-term implications for improving productivity. Fortunately, there is some limited evidence that such biases are receding, and that conventional agricultural intensification efforts are being modified to incorporate knowledge from farmers (Rhoades 1984). One project that experimented with women's knowledge in plant breeding involved selections of bean and cowpea varieties in Rwanda and Malawi over the years 1988–93. In an unprecedented collaboration, local women worked with scientists and anthropologists to develop a common understanding of their respective classifications of bean types and assessments of yield potential and other desirable cultural characteristics (such as faster cooking time) under actual growing conditions. In the collaboration, women farmers selected from more than 20 bean varieties those that they thought would do best under their growing conditions. They also grew those varieties that the breeders predicted would be more highly productive. The women's selections outperformed the breeders' selections by 60 to 90 percent, and they continued to grow these after the experiment was over. This is one of the few examples where women's indigenous knowledge was put to work in a way that combined local classification rules with access to new seed materials (Ferguson 1994).

Female scientists in developing countries also are helping to transform views of women's agricultural roles, arguing that the drudgery of women's agricultural lives needs to be changed, not defended. A celebrated and not uncontroversial example is Dr. Florence Wambugu, one of the first Kenyan women trained in biotechnology. To those who oppose chemical and biotechnological approaches to eliminating weeds of cereal and legume crops, she responds (from personal experience) that weeding is seasonal, back-breaking women's work throughout much of Africa. Over the past decade, striga, a particularly tenacious weed that is not easily eliminated by traditional manual weeding methods, has invaded grain crops and greatly reduced yields of maize, sorghum, and grain legumes. To those who lament the elimination of women's work by herbicides, Wambugu replies that the future for women in agriculture and food production depends on better science, seeds, and chemicals. In her estimation, the proper agricultural role for the new African woman in agriculture is in a genetic engineering lab, speeding up the breeding of new herbicide-resistant crop varieties that will make it unnecessary for African women now or in future generations to spend their lives pulling weeds (Gressel 1996).

What is being called for by innovative women scientists, farmers, and their advocates is nothing less than a revision of the development paradigm and women's roles within it. Only when women are scientists, planners, and extension workers as well as farmers will they be able to achieve full human rights, including rights to adequate food and nutrition and a sustainable environment. Only then will they be able to inject their special knowledge and energy into transforming agriculture and improving production.

Along these lines, certain nongovernmental organizations are attempting to change the ways governments, donors, and the people themselves look at their potential to transform women's lives and food insecurity. In addition to these efforts by agricultural, nutritional, and economic scientists, partnerships are growing between citizens' associations, both with and without the participation of scientists. South Asian nongovernmental organizations, such as the Bangladesh Rural Advancement Committee (BRAC), the Grameen Bank (which makes small-scale loans to women as part of a social-transformation program), and the Self-Employed Women's Association (SEWA, an Indian nongovernmental organization) are relatively large-scale operations that seek to improve women's lives, with particular attention to education, health and nutritional security, food security, and food production. The Hunger Project's 1999 initiative to draw attention to and empower the African woman food farmer adopts a different strategy, pressing African heads of state and their assistants into public statements that acknowledge the plight and the potential of African women food producers. This is not business as usual, but an unusual effort to join central government and women leaders with United Nations and NGO officials and individual donors who are mostly from developed countries, drawing greater attention to women as the potential solution for Africa's agricultural problems.

These are but a few examples of the kinds of coalitions, now available through improved communications technologies, that promise the 21st century might hold some very different and surprising possibilities for women, food, and even peace. This is not to say that all that is promised can or will be delivered, or that there are not countervailing tensions between developing and developed countries, and between women and men, over access to information and technologies, including the Internet. However, it does leave open the possibility of surprisingly positive scenarios in the face of the devastation of war, hunger, pestilence, and starvation.

Connections

To project the possible impacts of peace and of programs to enhance the capabilities of women requires creative thinking about food-security scenarios and policy tradeoffs. Shlomo Reutlinger, the economist behind the World Bank's 1986 study on poverty and hunger, later took his colleagues to task for not providing better understandings of the potential costs, benefits, and tradeoffs governing alternative policy choices. He emphasized how little economists know about the impacts of policy choices or investments in different types of social services, such as programs in women's education and health, on the alleviation of poverty, or the elimination of hunger, and on economic growth in particular national contexts. Although IFPRI economists, among others, are beginning to model some of the connections between women's education, food security, and nutritional outcomes (for example, Smith and Haddad 2000), there is still all too little policy- and country-specific data showing how particular policies make their impacts, or for that matter, what kinds of institutions should be involved in planning and implementing policies. Appropriate policy questions involve not only *what* should (or can) be done but *who* should do it and who should evaluate tradeoffs and then choose among benefits (Reutlinger 1996). Despite growing attention to the innovative programs and achievements of nongovernmental organizations, such as BRAC, the Grameen Bank, and SEWA, Reutlinger and others find there is still little formal understanding of the appropriate roles of NGOs in relation to governments or the private sector, for what types of programs, or in what types of environments.

A related problem is the lack of good information on what factors or conditions enable community-based, NGO, or pilot programs to be "scaled up," and, reciprocally, how large nutrition programs instituted by governments under the auspices of international banks might more effectively be "scaled down" to operate more effectively in local communities (Marchione 1999).

In the United States and in the United Nations, the terminology of "partnerships," and the need for more effective ones, are popular (for example, Eisinger 1998), but few studies show what makes some partnerships work more effectively than others, or how activities of governments and international agencies might link up more effectively with those of NGOs, the private sector, and local communities. In the developing world, for example, some multisectoral partnerships are widely cited as examples worthy of replication. These include the M. S. Swaminathan Foundation's biovillages (in India) and the Iringa community-based, integrated nutrition program in Tanzania (for example, WHO/UNICEF 1988). As models of government–community partnerships, however, they have not been widely imitated, and evaluations raise questions about the conditions under which particular programs succeed and the attributes necessary for their replication and successful scaling up.

Beyond partnerships, there are also a growing number of coalitions that hint at change in the way international development efforts are organized. One unusual coalition is building around opposition to the World Trade Organization, which unites diverse constituencies supporting economic rights, environmental protection issues (such as opposition to genetically modified organisms), and food security. These new coalitions and their channels of communication go beyond the microcredit, poverty-lending enterprise schemes, which in their time were also surprising success stories, to take local actions based on a global human rights perspective.

Transcending these technical and institutional issues, the major challenge for who will be fed is a cultural and moral one—whether the world will create a society that cares that everyone achieves a right to adequate nutrition and no one goes hungry. Whether scientists and the rest of the world arrive there safely and soon, on the basis of some of the technologies described in this session, will also depend on the ways scientists relate to society and its perception of risks and benefits. As Arthur Galston wrote 20 years ago, developing more thorough criteria for how safe "safe" should be is an imperative, as scientists create ever more complex plant-chemical systems. Science is not value free, and even those scientists who want to do basic research must involve themselves with the social consequences of their findings (Galston 1981). Equally, social scientists, as individuals and through their professional organizations, have an obligation to promote freedoms and prevent agricultural programs from interfering with justice and people's access to food, including the seeds with which they grow their living. Peace, and equal opportunities for women to participate in development and freedom, along with openings for innovative NGO actions, are just some of the surprise scenarios that could transform food-and-nutrition outlooks in the 21st century. As scientists and as human beings, we clearly have many underexplored opportunities to contribute to the way science can help more people feed themselves in the 21st century.

PART IV

Institutional Roles and Policy Priorities

CHAPTER 7

The Roles of Government and Multilateral, Scientific, and Private Institutions

EDITED BY NICOLE BALLENGER

Based on contributions from Alex F. McCalla,
Bruce Alberts, Donald Duvick, Eileen Kennedy,
Ellen Messer, and Craig Gundersen

A t the World Food Summit in Rome in 1996, the United States and 186 other countries committed to the goal of reducing by half the number of people around the globe who are chronically undernourished, and to do this by the year 2015. The number of chronically undernourished, according to the IFPRI estimates presented in this volume, is almost 800 million in the developing world alone. Clearly, we have an enormous job in front of us. Achieving food security for all households remains a challenge even in the United States, one of the wealthiest nations in the world (Nord, Jemison, and Bickel 1999). Food insecurity is not a problem limited to poor nations—it is a problem of poverty wherever poverty is found.

At a February 2000 symposium on global food security, the contributors to this chapter shared their views on the roles of their respective institutions in contributing to long-term solutions to global hunger and malnutrition. That day they offered their views on the contributions of the institutions they knew the best—that is, the World Bank, the U.S. government, the science academies, private sector agricultural research, and the nongovernmental organizations (NGOs).

Each of these institutions has a distinct and different comparative advantage in the global food-security arena. To ultimately be successful they must agree first on the most important steps to take and second on how each contributes most effectively to a common cause. This chapter emphasizes four central challenges for the combined efforts of public and private institutions.

Challenge One: Invest in Rural Income Growth

Empirical evidence in a growing number of countries shows that the most effective way to reduce undernutrition and malnutrition is through economic growth focused on the poorest people. In most developing countries that necessarily requires a positive focus on rural income growth in both the agricultural sector and the nonfarm rural sector. A positive focus means investments in rural education (particularly of women), health, water supplies, and infrastructure, as well as in technology to improve the productivity and profitability of millions of small-scale farmers. This is, of course, the case made by Ed Schuh in Chapter 5 of this volume. Yet it remains difficult to persuade general economists and country policymakers that a positive rural-oriented macroeconomic policy is critical. It is not enough to stop taxing agriculture with overvalued exchange rates and industrial protection or to remove cheap food policies and open trade. Macroeconomic policy must also focus on investments in public goods that facilitate rural growth. Despite rapid urbanization, the majority of the poor will remain rural dwellers well into the 21st century. The World Bank and individual countries' international development agencies, such as the U.S. Agency for International Development (USAID), have major roles to play here. However, despite major efforts over recent years to reemphasize this need, their encouragement of rural income policies is still spotty.

External experts who design programs of agricultural and rural investment in developing countries must take a more careful accounting of existing social, infrastructure, and resource fragilities than they have in the past. Working with local institutions and NGOs with local experience can help them avoid devising inappropriate strategies. Development practitioners and policymakers must also consider larger macroeconomic issues of how financial adjustments are administered, and trade liberalization negotiated, which may influence peace, poverty, and food security (Smith 1994; Stewart 1993). They must anticipate the effects of such policy adjustments on the poor before changes are implemented rather than trying to mitigate negative consequences after the fact. The development community now has enough experience to do far better at this than before.

Challenge Two: Enhance and Expand Safety Net Programs

Even with economic growth, the rural and urban poor will need safety net pro-grams that include nutrition and health services. These issues require major attention, especially in Africa and South Asia, if subsequent generations are not to be debilitated by the devastating effects of malnutrition and if the number of undernourished is to be significantly reduced.

Many possible solutions to food insecurity are proposed in this volume, including the expansion of markets and the increased use of biotechnology. Safety net programs will help ensure that these solutions are effective and, as important, will ensure that the costs of such solutions are not disproportionate-ly borne by poor persons. Thus, the continuation and improvement of existing safety net programs and the expansion of such programs must play an integral part in any comprehensive effort to alleviate food insecurity.

When effectively designed, safety nets can serve two primary roles in devel-oping countries. First, they can help ameliorate the negative consequences of economic growth for those who are temporarily harmed by changes in the econ-omy. These hardships can result from the consequences of more open markets or the business cycles inherent in all free markets. For example, workers in former-ly protected industries and workers who have lost their jobs during a recession may need food assistance for their families. In these examples, the recipients of benefits will probably need assistance for only a limited time, depending on the displacement of a new economy and the depth of a recession. (See Figlio, Gundersen, and Ziliak 2000 for more on the increased use of food stamps in the United States during economic downturns.) Second, for persons unlikely to benefit from economic improvements in either the short or even the longer run, safety nets can serve as a long-term source of food and the other goods necessary for survival. This role of a safety net is especially important for families living in rural areas of developing countries, which are often mired in persistent poverty without many opportunities, and for persons with characteristics associated with persistent poverty.

Safety nets may also directly and indirectly improve the long-term well-being of poor persons. Food assistance programs, for example, have a direct effect on the future human capital levels of children. Malnourished children and, more generally, hungry children have a difficult time learning in school, resulting in lower accumulations of human capital. The U.S. School Breakfast Program was established in lower-income communities in part out of such a concern. Many food assistance programs also have components that indirectly lead to long-term improvements. For example, the U.S. Women, Infants, and Children Program provides nutrition education and referrals to health-care providers. Another example is the provision of scholarships by Mexico's food assistance program, Progresa. School-age children who receive food assistance benefits through Progresa also receive money to purchase books and other school items. This program also directs more money to girls than to boys in an effort to reduce the education gap between girls and boys. (See Chapter 6 in this volume for more on the importance of women in maintaining food security.)

Challenge Three: Continue to Improve Food Availability

Food security is about availability of food, access to food and effective utilization of food within the household. The availability issue remains a significant challenge. In Chapter 1 of this volume Per Pinstrup-Andersen and Rajul Pandya-Lorch make a relatively optimistic case that on a global scale the world can produce enough food. But that optimism requires substantial increases in productivity (yields) because new land and more irrigation are unlikely to play a very significant role. Opening global markets to expand international trade in food is an important means of improving efficiency in food production and distribution, but a projected 2 percentage-point increase in global cereal trade, from 10 percent to 12 percent of production, cannot by itself solve supply needs in Sub-Saharan Africa or South Asia.

As Chapter 1 describes, 97.5 percent of population growth will occur in developing countries. The vast majority of that growth will occur in countries lying between the Tropics of Cancer and Capricorn. If global trade continues to account for about 10 to 12 percent of production, it means that most of the increases in food production needed for improved food security must come from farming systems between the Tropics. These tropical and subtropical systems are complex mixes of crops, livestock, and trees, often subject to extreme biotic and abiotic stresses and to water constraints and natural resource degradation. Further, agricultural scientists know much less about these systems than they do about systems in the temperate regions. And increasing urbanization in this region means that its population must increasingly buy what it eats in the marketplace, putting additional demands on the food production and distribution system.

Where will the needed expansion in food supplies in these regions come from? A portion of the increased supplies will come as farmers use more inputs such as fertilizer and water, and use them more efficiently. A substantial portion will also have to come from improvements in knowledge and technology. Although the private sector plays a dominant role in plant breeding in the United States and Western Europe, few private sector seed varieties are bred for developing countries. Seeds developed by the private sector generally do not fit the special needs of small (often semi-subsistence) farmers in marginal or otherwise unique growing areas. Maize hybrids developed by private companies account for about 15 percent of the maize area in developing countries. Private sector varieties of wheat and rice occupy less than 4 percent and 1 percent, respectively, of the area planted to those crops in developing countries. Private sector soybean varieties are important in the southern cone of Latin America but not elsewhere in the developing world. (See Heisey, Srinivasan, and Thirtle 2000 for a discussion of the privatization of plant breeding in industrialized countries.)

The development of private sector seed markets and industries in developing countries has been constrained by a number of critical factors, including the low incomes of farmers, small and differentiated markets, market and political instability, and the absence of effective intellectual property protections for seeds of self-pollinated crops. At the same time, funding for public sector agricultural research has been stagnating in both industrialized and developing countries. In industrialized countries the role of private sector agricultural research has expanded quite dramatically in relation to publicly funded research. Thus, the context for a discussion of the source of expanded food supplies in developing countries is one of an increasingly privatized system of agricultural research globally, where questions of incentives for private sector activity and partnerships in developing countries are still very much unresolved.

Biotechnology is one of several causes of the expanded role of the private sector in agricultural research in industrialized countries (Shoemaker 2001). Rapid advances in biotechnology, such as tissue cell culture, genetic engineering, and molecular mapping, appear to have made it more profitable for private firms to develop new crop varieties. So far, however, private firms have used these tools to develop traits of interest to producers in developed countries, such as herbicide tolerance. Ironically, the potential for applying biotechnology to improving diets and food security in developing countries seems immense, but the "privatization" of science, coupled with the now emotional global debate over genetically modified foods, threatens to prevent the needed application. No one knows for sure what the ultimate consequences of these changing conditions will be. But they may foreshadow the possibility of reduced progress in plant breeding for the next decade or more, and therefore reduced progress in the race to sustain needed growth in world food production. The World Bank, both directly and through its significant support of the Consultative Group on International Agricultural Research (CGIAR), has a major role to play in ensuring that developing countries have access to the best possible science if they choose to use it. We hope these choices will not be foreclosed by decisions in rich countries.

Challenge Four: Rethink the Roles of Institutions

The tasks of feeding a growing population and reducing undernutrition and malnutrition in the 21st century will have to occur under very different conditions than they did during the Green Revolution. Three critical differences are (1) as mentioned, most modern biological science is now done by the private sector, not the public sector; (2) economic policy is oriented toward free markets and open economies; and (3) decisionmaking within countries has become more decentralized and participatory. All of these factors, plus others, are significantly altering the role of the state. They do not make government less important but change its role from direct participation in and control of the economy to one focused on creating an appropriate institutional environment, pursuing non-distorting policies, and encouraging private sector growth through investment. In most developing countries there is no larger private sector than agriculture and agriculturally related rural enterprise. Changing the mindset of policymakers from one of direct government intervention and control to one of providing a nurturing environment is particularly crucial for providing food security for the poor. Again, the World Bank and international development agencies could and should play a substantial role in helping countries redefine the appropriate role of the state.

More careful consideration is required not only of what should be done but also who should do it (Reutlinger 1996). As discussed in Chapter 6 of this volume, despite growing attention to the innovative programs and achievements of NGOs, such as the Bangladesh Rural Advancement Committee (BRAC), the Grameen Bank, and the Self-Employed Women's Association (SEWA), particularly their participatory development activities, there is still little formal understanding of the appropriate roles of NGOs vis-à-vis governments (or vis-à-vis the for-profit sector). Likewise there is little useful information on what factors or conditions allow community-based or pilot programs to scale up and, reciprocally, how large programs instituted by governments under the auspices of international banks might scale down to operate more effectively in local communities. In the United States and at the United Nations, it is popular to speak of the need for more effective "partnerships." There are few studies, however, showing what makes some partnerships work more effectively than others or how activities of governments and international agencies might link up more effectively with those of NGOs, the private sector, and local groups. Efforts by donor nations to enhance the roles of NGOs and local groups—such as USAID's 10-year African Food Security Initiative, in which U.S. and local NGOs work to build Africa's capacity to manage its own food-security programs and policies—require more study.

The world's national science academies—which are NGOs of a special kind—should also be considered a potential force in improving food security. Although the science academies were founded to define, identify, and reward excellence in scientific research, today's academy meetings are likely to be about science policy, particularly about how the institutions can help their governments make wiser science-based decisions and help their societies use science and build science capacity more effectively. About 10 years ago the U.S. National Academy of Sciences started working with other academies to improve the effectiveness of the science academies worldwide vis-à-vis their governments. The idea started with a series of joint studies with Mexico, one of which was a joint study on the Mexico City water supply. That activity convinced the government of Mexico to start the equivalent of an academy advisory committee for Mexico, which is now operating as the country's national research council. In 1993 in New Delhi, most of the academies of the world met for the first time to address the global population issue. In May 2000 in Tokyo, a major meeting on the transition to sustainability included 80 academies. That meeting related directly to food security and specifically considered the role science and technology can play.

In early 2000 in Davos, 15 academy presidents met to create an Interacademy Council, which will do for the United Nations and the World Bank what an academy does for its own nation. Some of the issues for this new Interacademy Council are intellectual property issues, particularly North-South issues; capacity-building to use science and technology around the world; and the opportunities for enhancing the role of science made possible by the expanding Internet and the most dynamic of today's new institutions—the worldwide web.

Today's communications technology makes it entirely possible to develop a global knowledge system for food security based on new communications mechanisms. Such a system could disseminate knowledge down to the village level through a series of intermediaries and could allow scientists and others to hear from the village level what their needs are in science and technology and what they have to contribute in the way of indigenous knowledge.

Government, multilateral, scientific, and private institutions each have distinct contributions to make in addressing the challenges posed by food insecurity. Investment in rural income growth, improvements in safety nets, advances in knowledge for food production, and enhanced institutional collaboration are among the most critical of these challenges.

CHAPTER 8

Who Will Be Fed in the 21st Century? Solutions and Action

PER PINSTRUP-ANDERSEN AND RAJUL PANDYA-LORCH

With business as usual, hunger and malnutrition will remain prevalent and persistent. A food-secure world—a world in which each and every person is assured access to sufficient food to lead healthy and productive lives—will be realized only if:

- broad-based economic development is accelerated, particularly in low-income developing countries;
- investments in research, technology, and infrastructure are enhanced;
- women have a greater voice in decisionmaking at all levels;
- low-income people in both rural and urban areas, especially women, gain greater access to remunerative employment, productive assets, credit, markets, education, clean water, and health care; and
- armed conflicts and civil strife are limited.

Agriculture

The agricultural sector is central to ensure food security and good nutrition for all. Agricultural growth and development must be vigorously pursued to generate employment and income among the rural poor, to achieve solutions to grow-

Figure 8.1 Estimated contribution of major determinants to reduction in child malnutrition, 1970–95

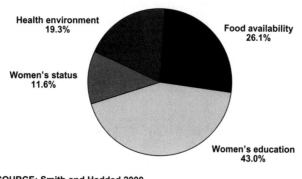

Health environment
19.3%

Food availability
26.1%

Women's status
11.6%

Women's education
43.0%

SOURCE: Smith and Haddad 2000.
NOTE: "Child malnutrition" refers to children who are underweight.

ing food needs and fill the widening food gap, to stimulate overall economic growth, and to ensure sustainable management of natural resources.

Agriculture is a major contributor to overall economic development in developing countries, especially the lowest-incomes ones, where it provides three-quarters of employment, nearly half of the gross domestic product, and more than half of all export earnings. In many countries, agriculture is the most viable—often the only viable—lead sector for economic growth and alleviation of food insecurity. Developing countries must take advantage of the opportunities offered by the agricultural sector.

Education, Health, and Opportunities for Women

With regard to which policy-related variables are likely to help improve the nutritional status of children, IFPRI research finds four critical reasons why child nutrition improved in the developing world between 1970 and 1995: improvements in women's education accounted for 43 percent of the total reduction in child malnutrition during this period, followed by improvements in per capita food availability (26 percent), improvements in the health environment (19 percent), and improvements in women's status relative to men (12 percent), as shown in Figure 8.1. Investments in these four areas could significantly reduce child malnutrition, but these investments will make little difference without improvements in national incomes and democracy (Smith and Haddad 2000). For Sub-Saharan Africa and South Asia—where the proportion and number of malnourished children are highest—improving per capita food availability and women's education offers the best hope for reducing child malnutrition in the future.

Comparing African countries that showed improved child malnutrition with those that showed worsening malnutrition leads to similar conclusions. The countries with improved nutritional status had larger increases in the enrollment of women in secondary school, in per capita food consumption, and in per capita incomes (SCN/IFPRI 1999). Furthermore, although women's status deteriorated in both groups, it deteriorated much more in countries where the nutritional status worsened. The data do not establish strict causality, but this analysis provides strong indications that women's schooling, women's status, per capita food intake, and per capita incomes are important determinants of child nutrition in Africa.

Conflict

The presence of civil conflict increases vulnerability to food insecurity, and vice versa (Messer, Cohen, D'Costa 1998). Recent information from FAO vividly demonstrates that the incidence of undernourishment or food insecurity is highest in countries with a high incidence of civil conflict. For example, 56 percent of the countries where more than half of the population was undernourished were experiencing conflict, while only 8 percent of the countries with the lowest incidence of undernourishment were mired in conflict (Figure 8.2). Similarly, child mortality rates are highest in those countries where a larger proportion of the population is undernourished; in other words, child mortality rates decline as the prevalence of food insecurity declines.

Research, Technology, and Productivity

With regard to sources for productivity increases in agriculture, consideration must be given to the opportunities presented by biotechnology, agroecological approaches, and information technology. Biotechnology, if appropriately focused on solving small-scale farmers' problems—together with traditional research methods, better agronomic practices, and better markets and policies—may help these farmers to increase productivity. Biotechnology may help them reduce production risks by making available crop varieties that are drought tolerant, pest resistant, and able to capture nitrogen from the air. Biotechnology that increases the content of iron or vitamin A or makes other nutritional improvements in foods may address serious and widespread nutritional problems among the poor in developing countries. Increased productivity will, in most developing countries, result in both higher incomes for small-scale farmers and lower food prices.

Figure 8.2 Food security, civil conflicts, and child mortality, 1990–96

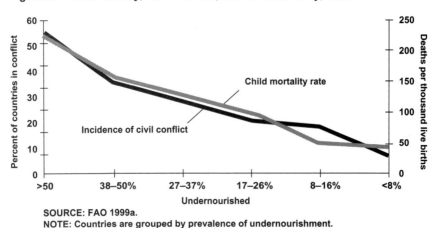

SOURCE: FAO 1999a.
NOTE: Countries are grouped by prevalence of undernourishment.

This is important for the poor, who typically spend 50 percent or more of their incomes on food.

Delivering the potential benefits of agricultural research in general, and of biotechnology in particular, to small-scale farmers and poor consumers in developing countries will require a combination of expanded public investment by developing countries and international agricultural research centers of the CGIAR as well as public–private partnerships. Governments in industrial and developing countries also have an important role to play in regulating the biotechnology industry. They must develop effective biosafety regulations, create and enforce appropriate intellectual property rights legislation, and enforce antitrust legislation to counter excessive concentration in the life science and seed industry. Relevant information on these issues must be made available to the public. If these steps are not taken, modern biotechnology will bypass the poor; opportunities for reducing poverty, food insecurity, and child malnutrition will not become reality; and the productivity gap between developing and industrial countries' agriculture will widen.

Information and communication technology (ICT) offers tremendous opportunities for reducing rural poverty in developing countries. Traditional information and communication technologies, such as wired telephones, fail to reach a large share of the rural poor partly because the wires are either not in place or not maintained in many rural areas and partly because existing institutions and rationing systems favor the nonpoor. Satellite-based cell phones and Internet access can bypass the rationing system and, possibly, the existing institutions that do not benefit the poor. At the same time, dramatic decreases in the cost of solar panels and wind energy make it feasible for the rural poor to power ICT—including cell phones, Internet access, radio, and television—with solar and wind energy. Access to ICT and energy opens up new opportunities for education, primary health care, and agricultural extension as well as for conveying information on markets, transport options, road conditions, employment opportunities, and other issues important to the rural poor.

Farmer Participation and
Sustainable Resource Management

Although the Green Revolution technologies have been responsible for enormous productivity increases among small-scale farmers in Asia, Latin America, and a few countries of Sub-Saharan Africa, many farmers have been bypassed. The desire to find ways of assisting these farmers, combined with concerns about excessive dependence on external inputs—such as fertilizers, pesticides, and irrigation water—embodied in the Green Revolution technologies, has stimulated interest in alternative or complementary approaches, including the so-called "agroecological approach." The agroecological approach aims to reduce the amount of external inputs that farmers have to use. Instead, it relies heavily on available farm labor and organic material, as well as on improved knowledge and farm management. One of the great strengths of this approach is that it promotes sustainable management of natural resources and active participation by farmers in identifying problems as well as designing and implementing appropriate solutions at the farm and community levels. Such participatory technology development can be extremely effective in finding the most appropriate solutions to production problems.

A large number of projects and initiatives have successfully applied agroecological approaches to expand yields and improve the livelihoods of farm families.[1] Illustrations from more than 30 African, Asian, and Latin American countries demonstrate the tremendous potential of agroecological approaches for promoting sustainable productivity increases in small-scale agriculture. While some approaches will have to change in response to increasing agricultural development and changes in farmer incomes and opportunity costs, such changes should come about easily as a result of farmer participation and leadership. Therefore, it is critical that farmers are, in fact, put in decisionmaking roles and that they are informed about their options for improving productivity, reducing risks, and increasing the well-being of the farm family. Such options should include access to external inputs and appropriate technologies to complement agroecological approaches. Farmers should not be made to suffer from the current debate over which approach is the most appropriate. Instead, farmers should be able to put together the most appropriate components from each of the various "approaches" in order to develop their own solutions.

Conclusions

IFPRI projections suggest that, under the most likely scenario, food insecurity and child malnutrition will remain widespread in 2020 in many countries, including most countries in Sub-Saharan Africa and some in Asia. Many millions of people will suffer from hunger and its debilitating consequences. This does not have to be so. A food-secure world will be within reach if revolutionary developments in information technology and biotechnology can be mobilized for the benefit of the poor and the food insecure in developing countries; if investments in the factors essential for agricultural growth—including agricultural research, human resource development, and strengthened agroecological approaches—can be renewed; if the political will to adopt sound policies for eradicating poverty, fostering food security, and protecting natural resources can be harnessed; and if behaviors and priorities can be altered to ensure sustainable development. This is not an insurmountable task. Great strides have already been made in reducing the burden of food insecurity around the world. Building on the progress made and taking the actions described here should finally enable realization of a food-secure world in the 21st century.

Notes

Chapter 1, "Meeting Food Needs in the 21st Century"

1. The Food and Agriculture Organization of the United Nations (FAO) classifies these people as chronically undernourished; that is, their access to per capita food supplies is less than 1.55 times the basal metabolic rate.

2. IFPRI's projections are derived from its revised and updated global food model, the International Model for Policy Analysis of Commodities and Trade (IMPACT), which covers 37 countries and country groups and 18 major agricultural commodities.

3. Malnourished children are those whose weight-for-age is more than two standard deviations below the weight-for-age standard set by the U.S. National Center for Health Statistics and adopted by many United Nations agencies in assessing the nutritional status of persons in developing countries.

Chapter 6, "Food from Peace and Roles of Women"

1. These themes are taken from the paper "Visions of the Future: Food, Hunger, and Nutrition," which was part of a workshop and World Hunger Report reviewing five-year progress toward meeting the goals of the Bellagio Declaration on Overcoming Hunger in the 1990s: eliminating famine deaths by moving food into zones of armed conflict, eliminating micronutrient deficiencies in vitamin A and iodine, reducing maternal and child hunger by half through improved programs of women's and children's nutrition, and reducing numbers of hungry households in extreme poverty by half through building on innovative poverty-alleviation programs (Messer 1996).

2. Data from FAO also highlight the significant relationship between hunger and conflict: more than half the countries with the highest incidence of malnutrition (more than 50 percent) are conflict countries, while those with the lowest incidence of malnutrition (less than 8 percent) also have the lowest incidence of conflict (FAO 1999a). In addition, data from the United Nations Children's Fund (UNICEF) indicate that conflict renders it difficult if not impossible for governments to organize campaigns for child nutrition. UNICEF's interim assessment of progress toward meeting the goals of the World Summit for Children showed conflict countries had not even taken initial steps toward country plans (Mason, Jonsson, and Csete 1996). There are also larger macroeconomic issues of how financial adjustments are administered, and trade negotiated, that influence peace as well as poverty, as witnessed in the 1998 uprisings in Indonesia. The association of conflict with forced repayment of international debt, structural adjustment, underdevelopment, and food insecurity point in both directions and suggest international institutions might do much more to prevent financial and trade policies from contributing to conflict (Stewart 1993; Smith 1994).

3. FAO data show that women account for more than half the agricultural labor required

to produce food in the developing world even though in most places, relative to men, they do not have equal access to land, irrigation water, technology, improved seeds, fertilizers, chemicals, or information. Speciosa Wandira Kazibwe, the vice president of Uganda, addressing the September 1995 Women's Conference in Beijing, noted that in Uganda, women produce 80 percent of the food and are responsible for 60 percent of planting of all food and nonfood crops, 70 percent of weeding, 60 percent of harvesting, and 90 percent of food processing and preparation by providing water and fuel. FAO aggregate data for Africa suggest that women not only perform seed selection; about 90 percent of hoeing, planting, and weeding; and 60 percent of harvesting, but also contribute about 80 percent of the work of food storage and transport from farm to town (FAO 1985). In Asia, women contribute anywhere from 10 to 65 percent of agricultural labor, and in Latin America and the Caribbean 25 to 45 percent, depending on specific crops and conditions.

4. For example, studies in pre-1994 Rwanda showed that cash income earned by women was positively and significantly correlated with household calorie availability (von Braun, Haen, and Blanken 1991); and even where female incomes were lower than total male incomes, no female-headed households exhibited severely malnourished children and proportionally fewer showed individual children who were calorie deficient (von Braun and Wiegand 1991). Female headship in poor households was correlated with better nutritional status for household and children (Blanken, von Braun, and de Haen 1994).

5. In traditional rural households women must often spend four or five hours per day acquiring fuel and water. Then, processing the main staple food and preparing supplementary relishes, garnishes, and beverages take additional time and compete with other activities at periods of peak demand for women's time allocations in agriculture, craft production, or marketing. Additional competing demands are child feeding, including breastfeeding, special preparation of weaning and children's foods, and children's hygiene, such as hand washing, clothes washing, and bathing. Time for preventive health care—such as immunization, growth monitoring, and nutrition education—compete with demands for income generation, food production, and household maintenance. Labor-saving technologies or commodities, such as substitution of kerosene for fuel wood, could remove much of the drudgery, but even where these are available they may not be affordable. The time-saving benefits for women's household activities may therefore be lost or postponed.

Chapter 8, "Who Will Be Fed in the 21st Century?"

1. These were identified and discussed at a recent conference, "Sustainable Agriculture: Evaluation of New Paradigms and Old Practices," sponsored by the Cornell International Institute for Food, Agriculture, and Development, Bellagio, Italy, April 26–30, 1999.

References

Alexandratos, N., and J. Bruinsma. 1999. Land use and land potentials for future world food security. Paper presented at the UNU/IAS/IGES international conference on a sustainable future of the global system, February, 23–24, Tokyo.

Anderson, M. B. 1999. *Do no harm: How aid can support peace—or war.* Boulder, Colo. U.S.A.: Lynne Reinner.

Anonymous. 2000. Population Facts. *Development and Cooperation 2000* 1: 7.

Besley, T., and R. Kanbur. 1988. Food subsidies and poverty alleviation. *Economic Journal* 98: 701–719.

Blanken, J., J. von Braun, and H. de Haen. 1994. The triple role of potatoes as a source of cash, food, and employment: Effects on nutritional improvement in Rwanda. In *Agricultural commercialization, economic development, and nutrition,* ed. J. von Braun and E. Kennedy. Baltimore, Md., U.S.A.: Johns Hopkins University Press.

Boserup, E. 1965. *The conditions of agricultural growth: The economics of agrarian change under population pressure.* New York: Aldine.

————. 1970. *Woman's role in economic development.* New York: St. Martin's Press.

Bowen D., T. A. Rocheleau, M. Blackburn, O. Andreev, E. Golubeva, R. Bhartia, R. H. ffrench-Constant. 1998. Insecticidal toxins from the bacterium Photorhabdus luminescens. *Science* 280 (5372): 2129–2132.

Brown, L. R., H. Feldstein, L. Haddad, C. Pena, and A. Quisumbing. 1995. *Generating food security in the year 2020: Women as producers, gatekeepers, and shock absorbers.* 2020 Brief 17. Washington, D.C.: International Food Policy Research Institute.

Bumb, B., and C. Baanante. 1996. *The role of fertilizer in sustaining food security and protecting the environment to 2020.* 2020 Vision Discussion Paper 17. Washington, D.C.: International Food Policy Research Institute.

Byerlee, D., P. Heisey, and P. Pingali. 1999. Realizing yield gains for food staples in developing countries in the early 21st century: Prospects and challenges. Paper presented to the Study Week on Food Needs of the Developing World in the Early 21st Century, The Vatican, January 27–30.

Chen, M. A. 1986. A quiet revolution: Women in transition in rural Bangladesh. Dhaka, Bangladesh: BRAC Prokashana and Cambridge, Mass., U.S.A.: Schenkman.

Conway, G. 1999. *The doubly green revolution: Food for all in the 21st century.* London: Penguin.

Conway, G., and G. Toenniessen. 1999. Feeding the world in the twenty-first century. *Nature* 402 (6761): C55–C58.

Crameri, A., and W. P. C. Stemmer. Combinational multiple cassette mutageneses create all the permutations of mutant and wildtype sequences. *Biotechniques* 18: 194–195.

Crosson, P. 1995. Future supplies of land and water for world agriculture. In *Population and food in the early twenty-first century*, ed. N. Islam. Washington, D.C.: International Food Policy Research Institute.

————. 1997a. The on-farm economic costs of soil erosion. In *Methods for assessment of soil degradation*, ed. R. Lal, W. H. Blum, C. Valentin, and B. A. Stewart. Boca Raton, Fla., U.S.A.: CRC Press.

————. 1997b. Will erosion threaten agricultural productivity? *Environment* 39 (8): 4–31.

Dasgupta, P., and K.-G. Mäler. 1994. *Poverty, institutions, and the environmental resource base.* Environment Paper No. 9. Washington, D.C.: World Bank.

de la Fuente, J. M., V. Ramirez-Rodriguez, J. L. Cabrera-Ponce, and L. Herrera-Estrella. 1997. Aluminum tolerance in transgenic plants by alteration of citrate synthesis. *Science* 276 (5318): 1566–1568.

De Soysa, I., and N. P. Gleditsch. 1999. *To cultivate peace: Agriculture in a world of conflict.* PRIO Report 1/99. Oslo: International Peace Research Institute.

den Biggelaar, C., R. Lal, K. Wiebe, and V. Breneman. 2001. Impact of soil erosion on crop yields in North America. *Advances in Agronomy* 72 (1): 1–52.

Donigian, A. S., A. S. Patwardhan, R. V. Chinnaswamy, and T. O. Barnwell. 1998. Modeling soil C and agricultural practices in the central U.S.: An update of preliminary study results. In *Soil processes and the C cycle*, ed. R. Lal, J. M. Kimble, R. F. Follett, and B. A. Stewart. Boca Raton, Fla., U.S.A.: CRC Press.

Downs, R. E., D. O. Kerner, and S. Reyna, ed. 1991. *The political economy of African famine.* Philadelphia: Gordon and Breach.

Dregne, H. E. 1990. Erosion and soil productivity in Africa. *Journal of Soil and Water Conservation* 45 (4): 431–436.

————. 1992. Erosion and soil productivity in Asia. *Journal of Soil and Water Conservation* 47 (1): 8–13.

————. 1995. Erosion and soil productivity in Australia and New Zealand. *Land Degradation and Rehabilitation* 6: 71–78.

Dregne, H., and N.-Ting Chou. 1992. Global desertification dimensions and costs. In *Degradation and restoration of arid lands.* Lubbock, Tex., U.S.A.: Texas Tech University.

Duvick, D.N. 1999. How much caution in the fields? *Science* 286 (5439): 418–419.

Eisinger, P. K. 1998. *Toward an end to hunger in America.* Washington, D.C.: Brookings Institution.

Engelman, R. and P. LeRoy. 1993. *Sustaining water: Population and the future of renewable water supplies.* Washington, D.C.: Population Action International.

ERS (Economic Research Service, U.S. Department of Agriculture). 2000. *Food Security Assessment.* Report No. GFA-12, Washington D.C.: Economic Research Service, U.S. Department of Agriculture.

————. 1995. *Conserving land: Population and sustainable food production.* Washington, D.C.: Population Action International.

Fahnestock, P., R. Lal, and G.F. Hall. 1995. Land use and erosional effects on two Ohio Alfisols. II. Crop yields. *Journal of Sustainable Agriculture* 7 (213): 85–100.

FAO (Food and Agriculture Organization of the United Nations). 1985. *Women and developing agriculture.* Rome.

————. 1990. *Water and sustainable agricultural development.* Rome.

————. 1996a. *Food, agriculture, and food security: Developments since the world food conference and prospects.* World Food Summit Technical Background Document 1. Rome.

————. 1996b. *Production Yearbook.* Rome.

————. 1997. FAOSTAT database <http://faostat.fao.org>, accessed March 1997.

————. 1998. *International Workshop on Developing Institutional Agreements and Capacity to Assist Farmers in Disaster Situations to Restore Agricultural Systems and Seed Security Activities. Project GCP/INT/660/NOR. Proceedings.* Rome.

————. 1999a. *Assessment of the world food security situation.* Report No. CFS: 99/2 of the 25th Session of the Committee on World Food Security, Rome, May 31–June 2. Rome.

————. 1999b. *The state of food insecurity in the world.* Rome.

————. 2000. *The state of food and agriculture.* Rome.

Fausey, N. R., and R. Lal. 1989. Drainage-tillage effects on Crosby-Kokomo soil association in Ohio. II. Soil temperature regime and infiltrability. *Soil Technology* 2: 371–383.

Ferguson, A. 1994. Gendered science: A critique of agriculture and development. *American Anthropologist* 96: 540–552.

Figlio, D., C. Gundersen, and J. Ziliak. 2000. The effects of the macroeconomy and welfare reform on food stamp caseloads. *American Journal of Agricultural Economics* 82 (3): 635–641.

Frewer L. J, C. Howard, R. Shepherd. 1997. Public concerns in the United Kingdom about general and specific applications of genetic engineering: Risk, Benefit and Ethics. *Science, Technology and Human Values* 22 (1): 98–124.

Frey, K. J. 1996. *National plant breeding study-1: Human and financial resources devoted to plant breeding research and development in the United States in 1994.* Special Report 98. Ames, Iowa, U.S.A.: Iowa Agriculture and Home Economics Experiment Station.

Galston, A. W. 1981. *Green wisdom: The inside story of plant life.* New York: Basic Books.

Gardner-Outlaw, T., and R. Engelman. 1997. *Sustaining water: Easing scarcity.* Washington, D.C.: Population Action International.

Glewwe, P. 1992. Targeting assistance to the poor: Efficient allocation of transfers when household income is not observed. *Journal of Development Economics* 38 (2): 297–321.

Gonsalves, D. 1998. Control of papaya ringspot virus in papaya: A case study. In *Annual review of phytopathology*, Vol. 36, ed. R. K. Webster, G. Shaner, and N. K. Van Alfen. Palo Alto, Cal., U.S.A.: Annual Reviews.

Government of Tanzania, WHO, and UNICEF. The Joint WHO/UNICEF Nutrition Support Programme in Iringa, Tanzania, 1983–1988: Evaluation Report. Dar es Slaam: Government of Tanzania, 1988.

Gressel, J. 1996. Plant biotechnology can quickly offer solutions to hunger in Africa. *The Scientist* 10 (19): 10.

Grosh, M. 1995. *Administering targeted social programs in Latin America.* Washington, D.C.: World Bank.

Gundersen, C., M. Yañez, C. Valdes, and B. Kuhn. 2000. *A comparison of food assistance programs in Mexico and the United States.* Food Assistance and Nutrition Research Program Report No. 6. Washington, D.C.: Economic Research Service, U.S. Department of Agriculture.

Gupta, R. K., and I. P. Abrol. 1990. Salt-affected soils: Their reclamation and management for crop production. *Advances in Soil Science* 11: 223–287.

Guyer, J. 1998. *An African niche economy: Farming to feed Ibadan.* Edinburgh: Edinburgh University Press.

Håkansson, I., W. B. Voorhees, and H. Riley. 1988. Vehicle and wheel factors influencing soil compaction and crop response in different traffic regimes. *Soil and Tillage Research* 11 (4): 259–268.

Hallman, W. K. 1996. Public perceptions of biotechnology: Another look. *Bio/Technology* 14 (1): 35–38.

Heisey, P., C. S. Srinivasan, and C. Thirtle. 2000. Privatization of plant breeding in industrialized countries: Causes, consequences, and the public sector response. Paper prepared for the 24th International Conference of Agricultural Economists, Berlin, August 13–18.

Herrera-Estrella, L. 1999. Transgenic plants for tropical regions: Some considerations about their development and their transfer to the small-scale farmer. *Proceedings of the National Academy of Sciences U.S.A.* 96 (11): 5978–5981.

Hobbs, P., and M. Morris. 1996. Meeting South Asia's future food requirements from rice-wheat cropping systems: Priority issues facing researchers in the post-Green Revolution era. CIMMYT Natural Resources Group Paper No. 96–01. Mexico City: International Maize and Wheat Improvement Center (CIMMYT).

Hong, T. D., F. R. Minchin, and R. J. Summerfield. 1977. Recovery of nodulated cowpea plants from waterlogging during vegetative growth. *Plant and Soil* 48: 661–672.

Hopkins, J. W., G. D. Schnitkey, B. L. Sohngen, M. J. Miranda, and L. G. Tweeten. 1998. Optimal cropland degradation with reversible and irreversible components. Paper presented at the Annual Meeting of the American Agricultural Economics Association, Salt Lake City, Utah, August 2–5.

Houghton, R. A. 1994. The worldwide extent of land-use change. *BioScience* 44 (5): 305–313.

ICAR (Indian Council of Agricultural Research). 1998. *Decline in crop productivity in Haryana and Punjab: Myth or reality.* New Delhi.

ICN (International Conference on Nutrition). 1992. *World declaration and plan of action on nutrition.* Rome: Food and Agricultural Organization of the United Nations.

IFPRI (International Food Policy Research Institute). 2000. Global study reveals new warning signals: Degraded agricultural lands threaten world's food production capacity. News release, May 21.

IWG/ FSAC (Interagency Working Group on Food Security and the Food Security Advisory Committee of the Board for International Food and Agricultural Development). 1999. *U.S. action plan on food security: Solutions to hunger.* Washington, D.C.: U.S. Department of Agriculture, Foreign Agricultural Service.

Jacoby, H. 1997. Self-selection and the redistributive impact of in-kind transfers: An econometric analysis. *Journal of Human Resources* 32 (2): 233–249.

James, C. 1998. *Global review of commercialized transgenic crops: 1998.* ISAAA

Briefs No. 8. Ithaca, N.Y., U.S.A.: International Service for Acquisition of Agri-biotech Applications (ISAAA).

Jefremovas, V. 1991. Loose women, virtuous wives, and timid virgins: Gender and the control of resources in Rwanda. *Canadian Journal of African Studies* 25 (3): 378–95.

Kaihura, F. B., I. Kullaya, M. Kilasara, R. Lal, B. R. Singh, and J. B. Aune. 1996. Topsoil thickness effects on soil properties and maize yield in three ecore-gions of Tanzania. *Journal of Sustainable Agriculture* 9 (1): 11–30.

Kayombo, B., and R. Lal. 1986. Effects of soil compaction by rolling on soil structure and development of maize in no till and plowing systems in a trop-ical alfisol. *Soil and Tillage Research* 7: 117–134.

Kilasara, M., F. B. Kaihura, I. K. Kullaya, J. B. Aune, B. R. Singh, and R. Lal. 1995. Impact of past erosion on land productivity in selected ecoregions of Tanzania. *Norwegian Journal of Agricultural Science*, Supplement 21: 99–106.

Knox, A., R. Meinzen-Dick, and P. Hazell. 1999. *Property rights, collective action, and technologies for natural resource management.* Washington, D.C.: International Food Policy Research Institute.

Lal, R. 1981a. Clearing a tropical forest. II. Effects on crop performance. *Field Crops Research* 4: 345–354.

———. 1981b. Soil erosion problems on Alfisols in western Nigeria. VI. Effects of erosion on experimental plots. *Geoderma* 25: 215–230.

———. 1987. Effects of soil erosion on crop productivity. *Critical Reviews in Plant Sciences* 5 (4): 303–367.

———. 1993. Tillage effects on soil degradation, soil resilience, soil quality and sustainability. *Soil and Tillage Research* 27: 1–8.

———. 1995. Erosion-crop productivity relationships for soils of Africa. *Soil Science Society of America Journal* 59 (3): 661–667.

———. 1996a. Deforestation and land use effects on soil degradation and reha-bilitation in western Nigeria. II. Soil chemical properties. *Land Degradation and Rehabilitation* 7: 87–98.

———. 1996b. Axle load and tillage effects on crop yields on a Mollic Ochra-qualf in northwest Ohio. *Soil and Tillage Research* 37: 143–160.

———. 1998. Soil erosion impact on agronomic productivity and environmen-tal quality. *Critical Reviews in Plant Sciences* 17: 319–464.

———. 1999. Soil management and restoration for C sequestration to mitigate the accelerated greenhouse effect. *Progress in Environmental Science* 1: 307–326.

———. 2000. World cropland soils as a source or sink for atmospheric carbon. *Advances in Agronomy* 71: 145–191.

Lal, R., and D. J. Cummings. 1979. Clearing a tropical forest. I. Effects on soil and microclimate. *Field Crops Research* 2: 91–107.

Lal, R., and G. S. Taylor. 1969. Drainage and nutrient effects in a field lysimeter study. I. Corn yield and soil conditions. *Soil Science Society of America Proceedings* 33: 937–941.

Lappe, F. M., J. Collins, and P. Rosset. 1998. *World hunger: Twelve myths.* New York: Grove Press.

Leisinger, K. M. 2000. Population growth, food security and civil society: The hunger problem can be solved. *Development and Cooperation* 1 (Jan.–Feb.): 8–12.

Leontief, W. 1953. Domestic production and foreign trade: The American capital position re-examined. *Proceedings of the American Philosophical Society* 97 (September).

Marchione, T., ed. 1998. *Scaling up, scaling down.* Amsterdam: Gordon and Breach.

Mason, J., U. Jonsson, and J. Csete. 1996. Is childhood malnutrition being overcome? In *The hunger report:1995,* ed. E. Messer and P. Uvin. Yverdon, Switzerland: Gordon and Breach.

McGaughey, W. H., F. Gould, and W. Gelernter. 1998. Bt resistance management. *Nature Biotechnology* 16 (2): 144–146.

Messer, E. 1996. Visions of the future: Food, hunger, and nutrition. *The hunger report: 1995,* ed. E. Messer and P. Uvin. Yverdon, Switzerland: Gordon and Breach.

Messer, E., M. J. Cohen, and J. D'Costa. 1998. *Food from peace: Breaking the links between conflict and hunger.* 2020 Vision Discussion Paper 24. Washington, D.C.: International Food Policy Research Institute.

Minchin, F. R., R. J. Summerfield, A. R. J. Eaglesham, and K. A. Stewart. 1977. Effect of short-term waterlogging on growth and yield of cowpea. *Journal of Agricultural Science* 90: 355–366.

Newbury, C. 1992. Rwanda: Recent debates over governance and rural development. In *Governance and politics in Africa,* ed. G. Hyden and M. Bratton. Boulder, Colo., U.S.A.: Lynne Reinner.

Nord, M., K. Jemison, and G. Bickel. 1999. *Measuring food security in the United States: Prevalence of food insecurity and hunger, by state, 1996–1998.* Food Assistance and Nutrition Research Report No. 2. Washington, D.C.: Economic Research Service, U.S. Department of Agriculture.

Oldeman, L. R. 1994. The global extent of soil degradation. In *Soil resilience and sustainable land use,* ed. D. J. Greenland and I. Szabolcs. Wallingford, U.K.: CAB International.

————. 1998. *Soil degradation: A threat to food security.* ISRIC Report 98/01.

Wageningen, the Netherlands: International Soil Reference Information Center.

Oldeman, L. R., R. T. A. Hakkeling, and W. G. Sombroek. 1991. *World map of the status of human-induced soil degradation*. Wageningen, the Netherlands: International Soil Reference Information Center and United Nations Environment Programme.

———— 1991. *World map of the status of human-induced soil degradation: An explanatory note*. Wageningen, the Netherlands: International Soil Reference Information Center.

Pagiola, S. 1999. *The global environmental benefits of land degradation control on agricultural land*. Environment Paper No. 16. Washington, D.C.: World Bank.

Pinstrup-Andersen, P., and R. Pandya-Lorch. 1994. *Alleviating poverty, intensifying agriculture, and effectively managing natural resources*. 2020 Vision Discussion Paper 1. Washington, D.C.: International Food Policy Research Institute.

Pinstrup-Andersen, P., R. Pandya-Lorch, and M. W. Rosegrant. 1999. *World food prospects: Critical issues for the early twenty-first century*. 2020 Vision Food Policy Report. Washington, D.C.: International Food Policy Research Institute.

Postel, S. 1999. *Pillars of sand: Can the irrigation miracle last?* New York: W.W. Norton & Co.

Quisumbing, A. R., L. R. Brown, H. S. Feldstein, L. Haddad, and C. Pena. 1995. *Women: The key to food security*. Food Policy Report. Washington, D.C.: International Food Policy Research Institute.

Ravallion, M. 1998. Land-contingent poverty alleviation schemes. *World Development* 17 (8): 1223–1233.

Ravallion, M., and K. Chao. 1989. Targeted policies for poverty alleviation under imperfect information: Algorithms and applications. *Journal of Policy Modeling* 11 (2): 213–224.

Reutlinger, S. 1996. Discussion—Is economic growth really the remedy for overcoming hunger and poverty? In *The hunger report:1995,* ed. E. Messer and P. Uvin. Yverdon, Switzerland: Gordon and Breach.

Rhoades, R. 1984. *Agricultural anthropology*. Lima, Peru: International Potato Center.

Rhoton, F. E. and D. D. Tyler. 1990. Erosion-induced changes in properties of a Fragipan soil. *Soil Science Society of America Journal* 54: 223–228.

Rivera-Bustamante, R. 1995. An example of transfer of proprietary technology from the private sector to a developing country. In *Plant biotechnology transfer to developing countries,* ed. D. Altman and S. R. G. Watanabe. Austin,

Tex., U.S.A.: Landes.

Rodgers, J., and J. Rodgers. 1992. Chronic poverty in the United States. *Journal of Human Resources* 28 (1): 25–54.

Rosegrant, M. W., C. Ringler, and R. V. Gerpacio. 1999. Water and land resources and global food supply. In *Food security, diversification, and resource management: Refocusing the role of agriculture?* ed. G. H. Peters and J. von Braun. Proceedings of the 23rd International Conference of Agricultural Economists, Sacramento, California, August 10–16, 1997. Aldershot, U.K.: Ashgate.

Scherr, S. J. 1999. *Soil degradation: A threat to developing-country food security by 2020?* 2020 Vision Discussion Paper 27. Washington, D.C.: International Food Policy Research Institute.

Scherr, S. J., and S. Yadav. 1996. *Land degradation in the developing world: Implications for food, agriculture, and the environment to 2020.* 2020 Vision Discussion Paper 14. Washington, D.C.: International Food Policy Research Institute.

Schuh, G. E. 2000. The household: The neglected link in research and programs for poverty alleviation. *Food Policy* 25 (3): 233–241.

SCN/IFPRI (Subcommittee on Nutrition of the United Nations Administrative Committee on Coordination/International Food Policy Research Institute). 1999. *Fourth report on the world nutrition situation.* Washington, D.C.

Sen, A. 1981. *Poverty and famines.* Oxford: Clarendon Press.

———. 1999. *Development as freedom.* New York: Knopf.

Shoemaker, R., ed. 2001. *Economic issues in agricultural biotechnology.* Agriculture Information Bulletin No. 762. Washington, D.C.: Economic Research Service, U.S. Department of Agriculture.

Smedema, L. K. 1990. *Proceedings of Symposium on Land Drainage and Salinity Control in Arid and Semi-Arid Regions, Cairo.* Egypt: Nubar Printing House.

Smith, D. 1994. *War, peace, and third world development.* Occasional Paper 16. Oslo, Norway: International Peace Research Institute, Human Development Report Office.

Smith, L., and L. Haddad. 2000. *Overcoming child malnutrition in developing countries: Past achievements and future choices.* 2020 Vision Discussion Paper 30. Washington, D.C.: International Food Policy Research Institute.

Soane, B. D. and C. Van Ouwerkerk, eds. 1994. *Soil compaction in crop production.* Amsterdam: Elsevier.

Soule, M. J., A. Tegene, and K. D. Wiebe. 2000. Land tenure and the adoption of conservation practices. *American Journal of Agricultural Economics* 82 (4): 993–1005.

Stemmer, W. P. C. 1994. Rapid evolution of a protein in vitro by DNA shuffling. *Nature.* 370: 389–391.

Stewart, F. 1993. War and underdevelopment: Can economic analysis help reduce the costs? *Journal of International Development* 5 (4): 357–380.

Swaminathan, M. S. 2000. Science in response to basic human needs. *Science* 287 (5452): 425.

Tanksley, S. D., and S. R. McCouch. 1997. Seed banks and molecular maps: Unlocking genetic potential from the wild. *Science* 277 (5329): 1063–1066.

Trewavas, A. J. 2001. The population/biodiversity paradox: Agricultural efficiency to save wilderness. *Plant Physiology* 125 (1): 174–179.

United Nations. 1996. *World urbanization prospects: The 1996 revision.* New York.

————. 1999. *World population prospects: The 1998 revision.* New York.

Van Lynden, G. W. G., and L. R. Oldeman. 1997. *The assessment of the status of human induced soil degradation.* Wageningen, The Netherlands: International Soil Reference Information Center.

von Braun, J., H. de Haen, and J. Blanken. 1991. *Commercialization of agriculture under population pressure: Effects on production, consumption, and nutrition in Rwanda.* Research Report 85. Washington, D.C.: International Food Policy Research Institute.

von Braun, J., and G. Wiegand-Jahn. 1991. Income sources and income uses of the malnourished poor in northwest Rwanda. In *Income sources of malnourished people in rural areas: Microlevel information and policy implications,* ed. J. von Braun and R. Pandya-Lorch. Working Paper on Commercialization of Agriculture and Nutrition No. 5. Washington, D.C.: International Food Policy Research Institute.

Voorhees, W. B., J. F. Johnson, G. W. Randall and W. W. Nelson. 1989. Corn growth and yield as affected by surface and subsoil compaction. *Agronomy Journal* 81: 294–303.

Wambugu, F. 1999. Why Africa needs agricultural biotech. *Nature* 400 (6739): 15–16.

Wiebe, K. D., and R. Meinzen-Dick. 1998. Property rights as policy tools for sustainable development. *Land Use Policy* 15 (3): 203–215.

Wiebe, K., M. Soule, C. Narrod, and V. Breneman. 2000. Resource quality and agricultural productivity: A multi-country comparison. Paper presented at the Annual Meeting of the American Agricultural Economics Association, Tampa, Florida, July 31, 2000, <http://agecon.lib.umn.edu/aaea00/sp00wi01.pdf>.

Wien, C., R. Lal and E. L. Pulver. 1977. Effects of transient flooding on growth and yield of some tropical crops. In *Soil physical properties and crop produc-*

tion in the tropics, ed. R. Lal and D. J. Greenland. Chichester, U.K.: John Wiley and Sons.

World Bank. 1986. *Poverty and hunger: Issues and options for food security in developing countries*. World Bank Policy Study. Washington, D.C.

———. 1997. *World development indicators 1997*. Washington, D.C.

———. 1998. *World development indicators 1998*. CD-ROM. Washington, D.C.

Xu, Z., N. R. Fausey, R. Lal and G. F. Hall. 1997. Soil management and topsoil thickness effects on maize for two Tanzanian soils. *Journal of Sustainable Agriculture* 10: 43–62.

Ye, X., S Al-Babili, A. Kloti, J. Zhang, P. Lucca, P. Beyer, and I. Potrykus. 2000. Engineering the provitamin A (beta-carotene) biosynthetic pathway into (carotenoid-free) rice endosperm. *Science* 287 (5451): 303–305.

Zhu, Y., H. Chen, J. H. Fan, Y. Wang, Y. Li, J. Chen, J. X. Fan, S. Yang, L. Hu, H. Leung, T. Mew, P. Teng, Z. Wang, and C. Mundt. 2000. Genetic diversity and disease control in rice. *Nature* 406 (6797): 718–722.

Contributors

BRUCE ALBERTS is president of the National Academy of Sciences, Washington, D.C.

NICOLE BALLENGER is chief of the Diet, Safety, and Health Economics Branch of the U.S. Department of Agriculture's Economic Research Service, Washington, D.C.

DONALD DUVICK is former senior vice president for research at Pioneer Hi-Bred International, Inc., and affiliate professor of agronomy, Iowa State University, Ames, Iowa, U.S.A.

CRAIG GUNDERSEN is an economist in the U.S. Department of Agriculture's Economic Research Service, Washington, D.C.

EILEEN KENNEDY is the former Deputy Undersecretary for Research, Education, and Economics at the U.S. Department of Agriculture, Washington, D.C.

RATTAN LAL is professor in the School of Natural Resources, Ohio State University, Columbus, Ohio, U.S.A.

ALEX F. McCALLA is former director of rural development at the World Bank and emeritus professor of agricultural economics at the University of California, Davis, California, U.S.A.

SUSAN McCOUCH is associate professor of plant breeding and international agriculture at Cornell University, Ithaca, New York, U.S.A.

ELLEN MESSER is a Woodrow Wilson fellow at the Woodrow Wilson International Center for Scholars, Washington, D.C.

RAJUL PANDYA-LORCH is head of the 2020 Vision for Food, Agriculture, and the Environment Initiative at the International Food Policy Research Institute, Washington, D.C.

PER PINSTRUP-ANDERSEN is director general of the International Food Policy Research Institute, Washington, D.C.

G. EDWARD SCHUH is regents professor in the Hubert H. Humphrey Institute of Public Affairs at the University of Minnesota, Minneapolis, Minnesota, U.S.A.

KEITH WIEBE is an economist in the U.S. Department of Agriculture's Economic Research Service, Washington, D.C.